IT STARTS WITH A STEP

IT STARTS WITH A STEP

WALKING FOR A BETTER WORLD

CLARA CECIL

NEW DEGREE PRESS

IT STARTS WITH A STEP

Walking for a Better World

ISBN   978-1-64137-128-5   *Paperback*
       978-1-64137-129-2   *Ebook*

CONTENTS

"The journey of a thousand miles begins with a single step."

— LAO TZU

SO, YOU WANT TO CHANGE THE WORLD?

———

"You can't change the world, you know."

My mom's jaw drops. She tries to speak, but the words won't come out.

While out for a springtime walk in our hometown of Annapolis, she's just finished telling her friend about how proud she is of her daughter, a soon-to-be Georgetown University graduate, for her determination to make the world a better place. She wholeheartedly believes that her daughter will change — and is already changing — the world for the better.

How could you, an educated and sane person, believe that it's impossible to change the world? she wants to say.

"I'm sorry you feel that way," she replies instead.

* * *

"What do you want to be when you grow up?" read the prompt for my first grade writing assignment.

"When I grow up I want be the President, of the United States," I wrote in crooked pencil. "I'm going to appoint my dad to the Supreme Court. I will make my mom the ruler of the BMA. I will get to be president for four years, in a row. I will live in the White House. I will also make new laws."

Short, simple, and to the point — with a little sprinkling of nepotism, a few grammatical errors, and some unexplained acronyms (I'm still not sure what I meant by the "BMA").

While my classmates wrote about how they wanted to be teachers, lawyers, doctors, nurses, and a number of other noble occupations, I had set my sights on the highest office in the land.

From an early age, my parents instilled in me the belief that I had the power to make a difference in the world. I was determined to change the world in some way or another, and what better way to do that, I thought, than to be the leader of the free world?

Emboldened by my parents' belief in my ability to make a difference, I confidently asserted that I would be the first female President of the United States to my teachers and classmates and everyone I knew — admittedly, a small circle at the time. At the end of the school year, my teachers Mrs. Gabelman and Mrs. Troy, proud of my dedication to my lofty goal, named me the "Most Ambitious" member of the class. I proudly hung the certificate on our kitchen refrigerator, taking it as an early sign of my teachers' support for my future political campaign.

In subsequent years, filled with the wisdom and practicality of age, I concocted new plans for how I wanted to change the world. In third grade, I decided that I wanted to solve people's problems as an inventor, drawing up detailed plans for a flying car and a robot that would cook and clean. In fourth grade, I declared that I would be a school teacher, so I could positively influence kids in the way that my teachers had. By fifth grade, I had landed on the fact that I wanted to help people in times of crisis by being a lawyer like my dad.

My world was simple then. Living a blissful childhood in a small Maryland suburb, I was only vaguely aware of all of the problems facing the world. I didn't comprehend the complexity of many of the world's challenges, from climate change and inequality to conflict and unemployment. To me, changing the world and having power were mutually necessary: I thought that the act of being in a position of power would guarantee my ability to change the world, and I believed that the only way to change the world was to be in a position of power.

In my youthful mindset, changing the world would have to wait until I was older or more educated or more experienced or more powerful.

* * *

The problems facing the world today are daunting — arguably, even more daunting and complex than when I was in elementary school dreaming of taking on the responsibility of being the President of the United States.

Sea levels are rising. Polarization is increasing. More than a billion individuals are living in extreme poverty. Obesity is on the rise. Trust in institutions is plummeting to all-time lows. Inequality is reaching new extremes. And that's just the beginning of the work to be done.

In the face of these problems that threaten the safety, security, and even existence of our world as we know it, how could anyone possibly make a difference?

My answer: Walk.

I know, it sounds crazy. The very survival of our planet is at stake, and I'm proposing that the solution could be as simple as going for a walk.

In the following pages, you'll discover that walking holds the key to solving the world's most pressing problems. From fostering mental and physical health and closing gaps of inequality to increasing productivity and reducing environmental footprints, the collective impact of walking has the power to change the world.

* * *

This book is a marriage of two of my greatest passions: walking and changing the world for the better. Before beginning this project, I had viewed these two concepts on completely different planes. I'd never considered that walking could be the answer to my childhood dreams of changing the world.

Throughout college, I spent a significant amount of time both in and out of the classroom exploring theories of how to change the world. This investigation ranged from doing random acts of kindness to brighten individuals' days to working in the business, government, and non-profit sectors to determine the unique potential for each one to do good in the world. Through these experiences, I discovered that impact is not limited to any specific industry, job description, stage of life, or type of individual. Change is derived from the collective power of individual actions. Every day — just by being present in the world — each person has an impact.

Prior to writing this book, I never considered walking as something that could be impactful. It was something I did every day. Simply the way to get from one place to another. Nothing more than a necessary — at times inconvenient — part of life.

In reflecting on the role of walking in my life, however, I realized just how impactful it has been. It's helped me stay in shape, provided me with stress relief, allowed me to explore and learn about unfamiliar places, cut down my personal carbon footprint, helped me build meaningful relationships, permitted me to voice my opinion, and aided me in learning about and shaping the world around me. Without realizing it, walking has impacted nearly every aspect of my life.

And so, I decided to investigate the central question of this book:

How can walking change the world?

When I posed this question to nonprofit executive directors, urban planners, business executives, teachers and professors, students, walking enthusiasts, and everyone in between, I wasn't sure how they might respond. Skepticism? Surprise? Ridicule?

I was overwhelmed by what I discovered. I began writing this book with a vague theory that walking has the power to change the world. In the process, I learned about the ways in which people are already leaving incredible marks on the world through walking.

The central message of all of my conversations and research?

Regardless of whether individuals realize its benefits, walking is an inherently impactful mode of transportation.

This book illustrates the ways in which people of all back-grounds — regardless of their age, geographic location, race, ethnicity, sex, gender, ability, or any other factor — can make, and are already making, a difference in the world by walking. In the following pages, I will walk you through the stories of some of the people who are already changing the world through their footsteps. While these stories offer ideas for channeling your steps into change, it is ultimately up to you to determine what kind of an impact you want your own steps to make.

The subsequent chapters, or "Steps," (pun intended) are organized around three phases of impact: individual, group, and societal. In Steps 1 - 3, you'll learn about ways in which you as an individual can ignite change by walking. To start, in Step 1 you'll discover that every day you have the power to change the world just by walking in it. Step 2 will show you ways to improve your short-term and long-term physical health through walking, and Step 3 will teach you about walking as a tool for improving your mental wellbeing. After all, in order to change the world you have to be at your best, both physically and mentally.

In Steps 4 – 6, you'll learn about the potential for impact when multiple individuals walk together in a group setting. Walking promotes interpersonal understanding, as you'll read about in Step 4. When people walk together, they can amplify the power of their steps by voicing their opinions to enact systemic change (Step 5) and raising money to promote worthy causes (Step 6).

Steps 7 – 9 demonstrate the extraordinary potential for impact when a society prioritizes walking. Step 7 highlights how walking is a vehicle for advancing environmental wellbeing, while Step 8 paints a picture of the economic benefits of a more walkable world. Finally, Step 9 concludes that walking is the key to the creative problem-solving required to change the world for the better.

This is a book for the dreamers and the skeptics. For the people who want to change the world and don't know where to start, this book is a guide to understand the impact of walking and to learn how to channel your steps into change. For the people who — like my mom's friend — think that it's impossible to change the world, this book will show you that change is indeed possible and that it can start with a single step.

PHASE I

INDIVIDUAL CHANGE

STEP 1.

PLACEMAKING

———

A person will take an average of 216,262,500 steps in their lifetime.

Two hundred sixteen million, two hundred sixty-two thousand, five hundred steps.

That's the equivalent of walking five times around the equator.

With every single step, you transform a place just by being present in it. That's a lot of power. Simply by walking and breathing and interacting and taking up space, you are changing the world whether you realize it or not, through a process you'll soon come to know as placemaking.

WHO GETS TO WALK?

"Nancy needs a friend to walk her home, and she listed you as a contact," the doctor's office receptionist said. "Could you be here in a few minutes to walk with her?"

It seems like a simple enough question. But Georgetown Professor Sarah Stiles' friend Nancy is paraplegic, relying on a wheelchair to get around.

Professor Stiles didn't think twice about the request.

"Of course I'll walk her home," Professor Stiles replied. "I'll be there as soon as I can.

* * *

"Nancy needed a friend to walk her home. And so, I walked her home," Professor Stiles told me matter-of-factly, ignoring the traditional literal meaning of "walking" someone home.

In a book about walking, it's important to define what exactly "walking" means. This book considers walking in its broadest, most inclusive sense.

Some traditional dictionary definitions of walking are inherently exclusive. Dictionary.com defines walking as "to advance or travel on foot at a moderate speed or pace; proceed by steps;

move by advancing the feet alternately so that there is always one foot on the ground."

An alternative, more inclusive definition of walking provided by Merriam-Webster is, "to come or go easily or readily." However, this definition still doesn't fully encompass all that it means to walk.

Professor Stiles firmly believes that the word "walking" does not only apply to able-bodied people who can walk on two feet. Although her friend Nancy is not able-bodied in the traditional sense, she has been married, given birth to three children, and was the Chief Financial Officer of a company, all proving that her body is capable of incredible things. The bumper sticker on the back of Nancy's wheelchair aptly reads, "Attitudes are the real disability."

While Nancy is not mobile on her legs, she still has the same opportunity as able-bodied individuals to experience all that a place has to offer and to contribute to its unique identity and character.

My preferred definition of walking is one in which Merriam-Webster intends to define walking in the sense of a spirit: "to move about in visible form." For the purposes of this book, the most essential component of "walking" is the act of being physically present in a space. Whether the movement occurs via two feet or four wheels, walking encompasses all of the ways in which an individual is present and visible in a space, influencing the world and making a mark on a place in an impactful way.

In order to realize your potential to change the world by walking, you first have to understand your unique power as a pedestrian in transforming a place.

SHAPING A PLACE

"Look around you. Really look. Can you see yourself here?"

When I was touring colleges during my junior and senior years of high school, this became my parents' mantra.

All around me, from my high school's hallways to family reunions, I constantly heard murmurs of "safety schools" and "SAT scores" and "GPAs" and "deadlines" and "acceptance." While even a mention of the college admissions process in the United States can be stress-inducing, my parents were determined to take the stress out of my personal college application process.

Thus, the mantra.

My parents wanted me to find a school that would challenge

me to become the best version of myself. They wanted me to find inspiration and discover my passions. To join a community that would not only accept but nurture and embrace me. To surround myself with people who would strengthen me to grow as a person. To be empowered to change the world. To find lifelong friendships.

They wanted me to be happy.

So, after the standard, often clichéd, college admissions tours were over, instead of sticking around to ask the tour guides to wager my chances of getting into the school, we would walk around the campus.

As we roamed, I would observe the people I saw: *How were they dressed? Did they seem happy?*

I would observe their interactions: *Were they smiling at each other? Did students greet professors as they walked around campus?*

I would also try to leave behind these thoughts and observations and instead just let myself walk: *Did I fit into the rhythm of the campus? Did I feel like I belonged?*

What I found, however, was that I didn't feel comfortable anywhere.

I felt like an imposter. I didn't know anyone, and I didn't have the first idea of how to fit in with any of the campuses' cultures or unofficial dress codes. I felt lost. And, most of the time walking through the campuses' mazes of buildings, I really did have no idea where I was going.

When I toured my dream school, Georgetown University, for the first time, I experienced the same feeling of being out of place. Something about our large tour group snaking through campus against the traffic patterns of students heading to and from classes felt unnatural and disruptive. It was daunting to think that regardless of the college choice I made, I would have to move to a place where I knew no one and felt like an outsider on campus.

By the time I reached my senior year at Georgetown, I found that these thoughts could not have been further from the truth. Over the course of four years, Georgetown became my home. It was a slow process of getting lost on more occasions that I would like to admit, constantly meeting new people, and forcing myself to travel far out of my comfort zone. However, I found that Georgetown became one of the places on Earth where I felt the most comfortable and at ease. It would be a rare occurrence to walk any distance across campus without seeing at least a few familiar faces.

Despite my initial skepticism that I would ever find my way

around the school's many buildings, I came to know the campus like the back of my hand. When visitors walking around campus asked for directions, I confidently pointed them in the right direction, hoping that my friendly demeanor would help them too feel at home on the campus.

Along the way, I learned my own power in shaping Georgetown as a place. As a college campus, Georgetown can be a stressful environment, filled with students hustling from one place to another or walking with their heads in their phones. For this reason, in the fall of my freshman year I joined the random acts of kindness club, Georgetown Individuals Vocal and Energetic for Service, more commonly known as GIVES. Like the random acts of kindness it facilitates, GIVES's mission is simple: "Through intentional acts of kindness, we strive to create a culture of altruism and inclusivity at Georgetown University."

For one random act of kindness during my time in GIVES, my friends and I wrote messages of encouragement in chalk outside of the library and other buildings on campus, as a way of transforming the physical space to be less stressful. On another occasion, we wrote letters of appreciation to people who work on campus whose contributions are often underappreciated. I wrote mine to one of the workers — affectionately known to students as Ms. Frankie — at the on-campus Einstein Bros Bagels location where I ate breakfast every day.

With my appreciation note in one hand and a bagel in the other, I tentatively walked up to the checkout counter where Ms. Frankie worked. We rarely talked aside from a transactional "Thank you" and "Have a good day." After paying for my food, I handed her the envelope saying, "I just wanted to let you know I appreciate you."

A few minutes later, she walked over to the table where I was sitting alone.

"You don't know how much your note means to me," she said, a tear visibly forming in the corner of her eye. Giving me a big hug, she continued, "My husband's mom is in the hospital and it's not looking good. Your note made my day a heck of a lot better."

Based on her cheery persona, I never would have imagined that she was masking so much pain.

After that simple demonstration of gratitude, Miss Frankie and I began to greet each other as friends during my daily bagel purchase and when we walked by each other on campus. While random acts of kindness are easy to execute, my experience with GIVES taught me the power of individual actions — no matter how apparently small — in transforming a place.

Georgetown as an institution has existed since its founding

in 1789. In the time of its existence, buildings have been constructed and torn down, students have come and gone, and it has evolved as a place. At its core, though, the spirit of the school — grounded in the Jesuit values of service to others and a commitment to academic excellence — has remained the same. Still, the people who interact on the canvas of Georgetown's campus — from students and dining hall staff to professors and facilities workers — have the power to shape it every day, taking Georgetown's mission and making it their own.

As I discovered after touring Georgetown, not every place manifests itself perfectly on the first encounter. Each place is a work in progress, waiting for people to walk through it and exercise their own power of placemaking. Once you've recognized your potential to transform a place, you can start to channel your steps into lasting change.

THE POWER OF PLACEMAKING

"I was just going through the motions of my daily commute," Ted Eytan recalled.

In 2007, Ted moved from Washington state to Washington, D.C., to begin working as the Medical Director of the Kaiser Permanente Center for Total Health. Initially, he had decided to walk to work every day — instead of driving or taking the

Metro — in order to get exercise, clear his head, and benefit from the transportation mode's enormous health benefits. However, he soon found that walking the same three miles to and from work every day was becoming monotonous.

Ted, an avid photographer, decided to start taking a picture every day on the way to work to capture a physical representation of his daily commute. When Ted started looking back at each of the commute photos, what initially had seemed to be a monotonous daily routine took on a new degree of meaning.

He no longer only noticed the same static concrete sidewalks and office buildings he passed by every day. While he had thought that the urban landscape itself was the central character of the city, he recognized that the city itself forms the backdrop while everything else occurring in and around the city composes the foreground.

In one of the commute photos featured on Ted's website from January 2018, the Capitol Building can be seen sitting prominently at the end of a long boulevard. Cars are lined up heading down the road in both directions, and the headlights of some cars are still engaged, indicating that this must be a snapshot from his morning commute. Only a single cloud crosses the blue sky while the rising sun illuminates the Capitol, enshrouding the building with white light that fades into dark blue higher in the sky. A jaywalker near the foreground is caught in the act, while Ted observes from his standpoint on the median strip at the center of the avenue, presumably waiting for his own walk signal. The sun's rays illuminate the buildings on the right side of the street, a red "For Lease" sign on prominent display on the first building in line, while the buildings on the left side of the street have yet to be touched by the morning light.

In another photo taken in January 2018 — likely just a few days after the previous photo — the Capitol is again featured prominently, also nestled between two lines of buildings at the end of an expansive boulevard. This time, however, a red traffic light is central to the photo, and a single pedestrian traverses a crosswalk one block away from Ted. Cars and their headlights are less prominently featured, as they are all stopped by traffic lights a few blocks away. While the Capitol is indeed visible, it is masked by foggy, soft yellow light radiating from behind the buildings on the right and left sides of the street. A large white cloud rests atop the Capitol Rotunda, connecting the tops of the buildings on one side of the street to the other. Above the cloud remains the remnants of the deep blue night sky, with long lines of white clouds cutting across the canvas.

While it would be easy to write off both of these images as "Pictures of the Distant Capitol Building from Ted's Morning Commute," that description does not acknowledge everything else that came together to formulate what Ted witnessed in the particular moment when he snapped the shutter on his camera.

Through his daily passion project, Ted noticed that everything about a city is dynamic. Think of all of the circumstances that had to occur in order for each of those photos to exist in its exact state. Every single person in every single one of those cars had to leave their point of departure at the exact right moment in order to make it into Ted's picture. The clouds had to be moving and the sun's rays had to be shining in just the right way to create the effect captured in Ted's photos. Had he waited even a few more seconds to take either photo, that cloud might have floated away or those cars might have sped by or that pedestrian might have already traversed the street.

* * *

What Ted captures in his photos is the art of placemaking. Any city or town is so much more than just a collection of buildings and sidewalks. Through the dynamic process of placemaking, a community creates a location as a place with a life of its own.

"Strengthening the connection between people and the places they share, placemaking refers to a collaborative process by which we can shape our public realm in order to maximize shared value," states the Project for Public Spaces, a nonprofit that helps people create and sustain public spaces in order to build strong communities.

Placemaking allows you to re-envision the potential of every-day spaces to better serve your community. As a collaborative process, placemaking requires the participation of all of the people who live, work, and play in a space to recognize the potential for the place to grow and change — to be alive. From improving transit and promoting social networks to encouraging retail activities and facilitating aesthetic appeal, both tangible improvements and intangible characteristics define a place.

Walking in a place is the simplest way to participate in the act of placemaking. By walking, you can interact with your neighbors, become a more active community member, and brainstorm ways to improve the places where you walk. Being physically present in a space allows you to literally change the look and feel of the place, as the pedestrians in Ted's photos did. Walking gives you the opportunity to transform your world every day.

In this way, placemaking is the foundation of walking for a better world.

∗ ∗ ∗

If pedestrians promote placemaking, cars stifle it.

While Ted learns about and contributes to his community through his walks, the people in the cars featured in Ted's photos are just passing by. It's safe to say that the people riding in cars didn't take the time to notice all of the details of the Capitol scenes to the degree that Ted did while taking photos on his walking commute. The cars don't positively contribute to the community's sense of place, and you could say that they even detract from it.

Wouldn't walking be more pleasant without exhaust from cars, horns honked by irritable drivers, and vehicles speeding through pedestrian crosswalks to catch the last millisecond of a stale yellow traffic light?

Regardless of the normalized role of cars in today's world, Ted wholeheartedly believes that you cannot have an impact on the world unless you walk.

"Walking forces you to be visible in places you normally wouldn't be, and it inspires you in ways you never would have imagined," Ted told me.

Walking — and the placemaking it facilitates — is most impactful when it is made accessible to a diverse group of people who can interact with and contribute to a place. While walking alone and with friends are both valuable experiences, Ted believes that walking in the same space as people who are different from you has the potential to transform your entire worldview. On his daily walk to work he comes into contact with individuals of all backgrounds, and he imagines the unique stories of each individual as he passes by them on the street.

A shared space can have the effect of being a common denominator.

The Kaiser Permanente Center for Total Health where Ted works is located in the H Street Corridor neighborhood of Northeast Washington, D.C., a place made more walkable in recent years through infrastructure investments. Ted and his colleagues actively engage in the placemaking that occurs in the area surrounding the Kaiser Permanente office, whether it is by conducting walking meetings, commuting as pedestrians, or taking walking breaks during work. By walking in the community, they are better able to think about their own impact on the community, learn about the other people who live and work in the community, and contemplate how to better serve the community's needs.

Ted and the Kaiser Permanente team's mindset about community membership is a departure from the traditional American pattern of commuting. Traveling by motor vehicle, it's easy to get into the vehicle at point A and to get out at point B, without taking the time to fully experience the communities at either end of the journey or in the space between points A and B. Walking requires you to spend a longer period of time being physically present in a space, permitting you to both contribute to its sense of place and learn about its unique characteristics and needs. Instead of just observing a place, a pedestrian becomes part of the fabric of a community by walking.

While a city in its most literal sense is simply a collection of buildings, the buildings are just one part of the equation. When people take time to learn about and contribute to the communities where they live and work by walking, the collective power of people interacting in those places has the potential to change the world.

Still, there are obstacles that block individuals' ability to walk. As you'll soon learn, efforts to enhance walkability are a critical component of allowing more people to walk for a better world.

TOWARDS A MORE WALKABLE WORLD

"Why do you need a global strategy to put one leg in front of another?" Jim Walker was asked in the early days of his nonprofit, Walk21.

"What next? A breathing strategy?" another person scoffed at the organization's mission.

This skepticism of "walkability" is understandable. For many people, walking is a daily part of life that occurs without a second thought. *As long as people have legs and there is ground to walk on, there shouldn't be a need for an international non-profit entirely centered around walking, right?*

As you might expect from a book about walking, the answer is: *Not exactly...*

* * *

By virtue of his last name, Jim Walker was destined for a career in walking.

Early in his career, Jim worked as a park ranger in Great Britain's national parks. On a daily basis, he experienced and observed the overwhelming joy of breathing in fresh air and being surrounded by nature. Wanting to share the simple pleasures of the outdoors with the residents of urban areas, Jim decided to shift his career path and began working to promote walking routes in London. He hoped to share the restorative benefits of rural trails with the residents of one of the world's largest cities. Throughout his career, Jim has improved the quality of countless individuals' everyday lives through walkability, proving just how powerful pedestrians can be.

Through his work, Jim discovered that many factors serve to block individuals' ability to walk. As you'll learn in greater detail, factors such as income, gender, race, age, and ability can limit the potential of individuals to exercise their right to walk. On top of these individual factors, societal shifts towards increasingly sedentary lifestyles and a growing reliance on motorized vehicles have jeopardized the prevalence of walking as a mode of transportation. This decreased level of physical activity has negative implications for health, the environment, happiness, and the economy.

"Walkability is a word that did not exist just 20 years ago," said Dan Burden, the Director of Innovation and Inspiration at Blue Zones and one of the 100 Most Influential Urbanists of All Time. "We made walking so unnatural that we had to invent a word to describe what we were missing."

In 2000 Jim and two friends, Bronwen Thornton and Rodney Tolley, founded Walk21 with the goal of igniting a global movement around walking and walkability. Walk21 organizes annual conferences that bring together experts from different sectors, disciplines, and parts of the world. In less than two decades since its inception, Walk21 has evolved into a community of more than 5,000 people in 70 countries.

As an organization centered around walking, Walk21 has encountered its fair share of skeptics and critics.

"Walking is an unspectacular natural transport mode. So why is a walking policy necessary?" Jim was asked in one interview that I came across.

"It's not about walking," Jim responded. "We don't walk 50 kilometres a day — we are not mad. Walking is the indicator of livability… We found out that you can either measure a hundred parameters, or simply take a look at walking. How can I find out if one city is better than another? I sum it up in one point: if you have children, is this city really the place where you want to raise them, or would you rather move away? And when you are old and retired, will you move away, or will you stay? If it is a good place for children and for elderly people, then you have a successful place. If not, there is something wrong."

At the end of the day, Jim believes that walking is an indicator of quality of life. As a result, he has embraced walkability as his vehicle for change in making the world a better place.

While a five-day conference may seem too short to enact lasting change, Walk21 is committed to instilling a legacy in each conference host city. Each host city commits to an ambitious vision for what the conference can accomplish, agreeing to a three-year commitment to walkability that spans one year before and one year after the year of the conference. Walk21 is determined to understand and evolve each host city as a place, not just as a conference location. The lessons learned in each host city are channeled into new projects in cities around the world.

Walk21's 16th conference was held in Vienna, Austria in 2015.

"How about a budget of $500,000?" Jim and his colleagues at Walk21 requested of the city's mayor in the year of planning leading up to the conference.

"How about a budget of $5 million?" the mayor countered, indicating Vienna's substantial commitment to walkability.

If Vienna was going to commit to hosting the conference, the mayor was determined to do it properly. And that they did.

Vienna's strategy around walkability was three-fold: 1) researching motives for and obstacles to walking in Vienna; 2) improving the city's walking infrastructure, especially through sidewalks; and 3) implementing a communications strategy to encourage citizens to walk more. Critical for behavior change, the communications strategy included the distribution of walking maps around the city and the creation of the Vienna Walking App, which rewards citizens for steps walked in the city. To further incentivize walking among the Viennese, there were also free events and festivals centered around the theme of walking.

Implementing these ambitious goals required the commitment of the entire city, particularly government departments that had never previously collaborated with each other. By the end of the campaign, all of these activities resulted in an increase in walking in a city that was already very pedestrian-friendly.

The city's sustained commitment to walkability explains why Vienna has been recognized as the world's most livable city nine years in a row from 2010 to 2018, confirming Jim's stance that walking is an optimal indicator of livability.

✶ ✶ ✶

When they're not busy organizing conferences, Jim and his Walk21 colleagues use the organization's international reputation to promote walking among businesses, governments, and NGOs. As the leading international authority on walkability, Walk21 proposes policy solutions to governments and promotes walkability to the United Nations.

Jim's primary piece of advice?

"Just give pedestrians a bit of space."

The prospect of installing sidewalks throughout an entire city may seem daunting, but providing pedestrians with a place to walk could be as simple as marking a line on existing pavement. It's impossible to encourage people to walk more if they don't have the space to do it safely.

"Start with space," Jim advises. Then, behavior change and further investments will follow over time.

In Jim's ideal world, everyone would walk all of the time. But he's realistic, and he recognizes that enacting that kind of behavior change takes time. That's why Jim's primary focus at the moment is on where the most people are walking right now. And that's in low-income countries, where nearly 70 percent of people rely on walking as their primary form of transportation on a daily basis. The low-income countries where the most people walk often have the poorest walking conditions.

"We are failing each other," Jim told me. "We have all of these people walking, and it doesn't make sense to spend 80 percent of the budget to facilitate the 20 percent of people in cars."

Bogotá, Colombia, offers an example of how to get walkability right in the developing world. By the 1990s, the city had become hallmarked by pollution and traffic and was overshadowed by poverty, acts of terrorism, and the remnants of civil war. Beginning with his 1997 campaign, Bogotá Mayor Enrique Peñalosa has led the city on a mission to make people happier through increased walkability.

"As a fish needs to swim, a bird to fly, a deer to run, we need to walk; not in order to survive, but to be happy," Mayor Peñalosa said in his TED Talk, "Walkable Cities."

In his book *Happy City*, Charles Montgomery chronicles Bogotá's path to becoming a happier, more walkable city. Rather than investing in highways, Peñalosa prioritized investments in paths for pedestrians and bikes, parks and pedestrian plazas, and urban amenities such as libraries, schools, and daycare centers. By giving pedestrians the space they so desperately needed, the city began to see changes in its citizens' outcomes. Traffic fatalities decreased, the city's smog faded, and the people of Bogotá showed signs of being happier.

While the process was long and complex, the primary lesson to take away from Bogotá is that strategically implemented walkability is a legitimate investment that is capable of generating remarkable outcomes.

* * *

"If you take people on a walk, it generally brings out the best in people," Jim believes.

Placemaking occurs in a self-perpetuating cycle: a place becomes the best form of itself when people walk in it, and a lived-in place encourages people to be their best selves.

"We walk to be inspired by how to leave our mark on the world," Jim says, speaking from personal experience. When he walks in a place, he develops a fuller understanding of the place's positive and negative aspects. Confronted face-to-face with a place's challenges and shortcomings, he is inspired to think about how he could effect change in that space.

Transforming the way the world walks is not easy work. There are times when Jim has felt alone in his work to promote a more walkable world, and he's encountered his fair share of moments of self-doubt. For this reason, Jim is committed to creating a community of change-makers throughout the world. Bringing together like-minded people from all sectors and all walks of life, the Walk21 conference provides attendees with the support they need to change the world. The conference serves as a reminder that people all around the world are working towards the same goals of sustainability and equity, and thus inspires and empowers individuals to continue their impactful work. At the end of the day, seeing the results of his work around the world makes Jim's work worth it.

"Being inspired by the beauty of the great outdoors in the middle of the mountain or the top of a hill or convening with nature directly yourself is an awesome, uplifting, magical experience," he reflects. "All I'm trying to do is remind people that that is there in front of your face every day. If you're sitting in a café watching people or promenading up and down the street or just having to go to work, you can make that a moment in your day, not a chore. You can make that experience the highlight of your day, or you can make it your entire day, you can make it your job, you can make it your life. Because you realize that that's the bit that gives you the greatest joy."

Jim's work is a reminder that changing the world doesn't have to be complicated. Every individual has the opportunity to leave their own mark on the world just by walking in a place.

"People make places," Jim told me. If this is the case, then, a critical first step in changing the world is making places accessible for all people to walk in so that more people have the opportunity to exercise their role in placemaking.

COMPLETE STREETS

"At America Walks, we believe that every individual, regardless of age, ability, gender, sexual orientation or economic status has the right to walk and be physically active," says Kate Kraft of the organization's commitment to inclusion.

Kate Kraft is a nothing short of a rock star in the walking community, especially when it comes to accessibility. I asked each of the experts I interviewed for this book who I should talk to next, and on many more occasions than one I heard the enthusiastic reply, "You have to talk to Kate Kraft!"

As the executive director of America Walks, Kate forwards the organization's mission of empowering individuals, organizations, and businesses to walk more and to make the United States a more walkable place. In her role, Kate connects different sectors and disciplines to design a more walkable world for all people.

After hearing the glowing praise of Kate's work, I reached out to her to see if she would be willing to tell me more about her experience. Following a short email exchange with Kate herself, she and I scheduled a Skype call. Anxiously awaiting our conversation, I excitedly wrote down a long list of all of my unanswered questions about walking and strategies for making walking more accessible.

While learning more about Kate's background, I stumbled upon America Walks' vision of the world: "By 2030, streets and neighborhoods in all American communities are safe and attractive public places that encourage people of all ages, abilities, ethnicities, and incomes to walk for transportation, wellness, and fun."

At first glance, it sounds utopian. And somewhat counterintuitive. Walking is such a normal part of life for so many of us — how could something like walking possibly be unequal?

Indeed, access to walking is unequal based on factors such as age, race, ability, and income. According to Kate, communities where there is the least investment in walkable infrastructure are often the communities where people are less likely to own cars and are more in need of a safe, walkable infrastructure.

People who walk in low-income neighborhoods are twice as likely to be killed by traffic than those in more affluent areas. According to the report "Dangerous by Design," African-American pedestrians are 60 percent more likely to be killed by cars than whites, and Latinos are 43 percent more likely to be killed than whites.

Led by Kate Kraft, America Walks is making strides in realizing its vision of a more walkable world.

"Walking is not just walking," Kate told me. "It's a means of connecting people across all kinds of disciplines, communities, and interests to try to bridge divides."

To Kate, walkability isn't just a good thing to strive for — it's a moral imperative.

"The benefits of walking in walkable communities are so great that to deny someone access through poor infrastructure and disinvestment is really an incredible social justice violation," she informed me.

At the 2017 National Walking Summit, Kate and other leaders of implementing walkability in the United States convened in St. Paul, Minnesota, to build community and brainstorm ways to make walking more equitable. During the Summit, groups of wheelchair-bound attendees went on accessibility audits throughout the city. After spending an afternoon navigating the city by wheelchair, the auditors found that many of the city's sidewalks that were deemed "walkable" were only accessible by foot and not to people in wheelchairs.

Accessibility is a critical component of walkability. In order to create a more walkable world, walking has to be accessible to everyone — not just to those who walk in the traditional sense of the word.

"The places where we live, work and play result from a combination of deliberate decisions, financial allocations and political will," according to America Walks. "In many cases, these decisions have not produced 'places people love' nor developed vibrant, livable communities."

Every planning and infrastructure decision on the part of investors, policymakers, planners, nonprofit leaders, and pedestrians has the power to either reinforce inequality or combat it. For the most part, past decisions have reinforced inequality, resulting in many of the inaccessible communities that we see today.

In an effort to combat inaccessibility and inequality, movements such as Complete Streets are fighting for more walkable communities. "A Complete Streets approach integrates people and place in the planning, design, construction, operation, and maintenance of our transportation networks," explains the National Complete Streets Coalition. "This helps to ensure streets are safe for people of all ages and abilities, balance the needs of different modes, and support local land uses, economies, cultures, and natural environments."

Kate — a strong supporter of the Complete Streets approach — believes that safer, more convenient, and better designed streets make the world a better place for everyone. Creating a more walkable world is a matter of careful planning and purposeful infrastructure investment. It requires the cooperation of all parties engaged in the act of placemaking — including businesses, governments, nonprofits, planners, and pedestrians themselves — to make walkable places more accessible, more common, and better integrated with other modes of transportation.

"We need a surge in infrastructure spending but it needs to be the right infrastructure," Kate explained to me. "We want a balanced transportation system that provides infrastructure for safe, convenient and accessible mobility of all types."

Enacting this vision of walkability sounds expensive — but

it doesn't have to be. Instead of going on with infrastructure investments as usual, the same money that is currently spent on infrastructure can be allocated in a way that consciously makes people better off. As you'll learn in Step 8, these investments in walkability pay off greatly in the boost they give the economy.

It's a powerful thing to provide people with access to a place. Indeed, a place is incomplete if it does not include people of diverse experiences. Thus, walking — and the places where people walk — should be made accessible to people regardless of their ability, race, income level, gender, age, and any other factors. Making walking more inclusive expands the opportunity to all individuals to make an impact on the world.

———

Just by walking in it, pedestrians have the power to transform the world. How to use that power, however, is up to the individual. The following Steps will highlight ways to use the power of the pedestrian as a force for good, from encouraging physical and mental health and promoting environmental wellbeing to fostering understanding and boosting the economy.

STEP 2.

PHYSICAL HEALTH

———

"Je me suis cassé le pied. I broke my foot," I said to the doctor in broken French.

"Comment? How?" he replied skeptically to my self-diagnosis.

How? I thought to myself, pausing before replying to his question because the words were too difficult to utter out loud.

"J'ai trop marché. I walked too much."

The doctor's mouth formed an amused smirk at his young American patient's apparent stupidity.

In order to walk to change the world, I learned, you have to start by taking care of yourself.

* * *

During the summer of 2016, I studied abroad for six weeks in France through the Georgetown University French Language, Business, and Politics summer immersion program. We spent the first two weeks in Tours, a small city in central France known especially for its wine and cheese, and the last four weeks in Paris, arguably one of the most walkable cities in the world. While in Paris, I walked upwards of 20,000 steps per day, eager to explore all that the city had to offer. From sunset strolls along the Seine River to long days spent meandering through museums, whenever I was not in class or sitting at a café, I was constantly on my feet.

I quickly wore down the travel sandals I had purchased, which were minimally supportive to begin with. While I consider myself to be in good physical shape, the combination of my improper footwear and my sustained high level of physical activity proved to be displeasing to my left foot. On one of my first days in Paris, I returned home from a long day of walking to find that my foot was swollen, red, and painful to touch. Despite the pain of my injury, I created my own foot bandage with materials purchased from a local pharmacy and kept up my walking habits, determined to continue to experience the city in all of its glory.

Why on Earth did I keep walking?

In short, I was in love. Paris was a magical wonderland full of picturesque parks and admirable street style, bustling markets and captivating cafés, breathtaking boulevards and history come to life. The sights, sounds, and smells of Parisian streets cannot be fully experienced in any other way but walking. While I do love and appreciate the Paris Metro, I was determined not to spend my summer underground.

After two weeks of hobbling around the city, I started to worry that my foot pain had devolved into a legitimate injury. Searching online using the spotty Wi-Fi of my host family's apartment, I questioned Google: "How do I know if my foot is broken?" WebMD provided me with the preliminary medical advice I needed in my moment of desperation. Pain? Check. Bruising? Not particularly. Swelling? Absolutely. Can you hop on one foot?

This was the moment of truth.

I so badly wanted to convince myself that there was no way that I could have possibly broken my foot by doing nothing other than walking. I stood on one foot, channeling all of my energy into the muscles of my left leg, willing my foot to lift even slightly off of the ground. Despite my many attempts and admirable efforts, I could not pass the simple hopping-on-one-foot test.

At dinner that night, overlooking the twinkling evening lights of the Eiffel Tower from my host family's dining room, I timidly asked for recommendations for a nearby doctor.

"*Je pense que je me suis cassé le pied.* I think that I broke my foot," I told my host family with embarrassment, recounting the story of the gradual buildup of my foot pain.

My host parents looked at each other first with amusement at the foolishness of their American host student's self-diagnosis, then with genuine concern upon seeing my swollen foot. They wrote down the phone number of their family doctor on a piece of scrap paper, and I called to schedule an appointment the next morning. Later that day, I hobbled to the doctor's office, located less than three blocks from their apartment.

I was reluctant to go, as I could picture myself spending my final two weeks in Paris hobbling around on crutches or sweating through a boot in the summer heat. While I could proficiently hold a conversation in French in the realms of business, politics, or small talk, my knowledge of French medical terminology was nonexistent. Prior to my appointment, I made note of important terms in the "Notes" app on my phone: *une fracture de fatigue* (a stress fracture), *l'enflure* (inflammation), *enflé* (swollen), *radiographie* (X-ray).

Despite the language barrier and the doctor's amusement

with my situation, he proved to be a great help. He suspected that I had indeed broken my foot, but to know for sure would require X-rays and further examination.

"*Reste pour tes dernières semaines à Paris.* Rest for your last two weeks in Paris," he advised, instructing me to have a formal examination upon returning to the United States. While I was happy to hear that I would not have to maneuver through the city with a boot or crutches, this prescription of rest was not what I was hoping to hear. He gave me a medical band to wrap around my foot in the event that I did need to walk somewhere, and I journeyed back to my host family's apartment.

As you might have suspected, I did not abide by the doctor's orders. During my last two weeks in Paris, I kicked my walking into high gear, putting on my medical band and trying to crank through the list of things I had yet to see or do or experience in the city. While my leg muscles were indeed toned from all of the walking, the pang of pain that accompanied each step of my left foot reminded me of my physical limitations. Aside from the foot pain, however, my last two weeks in Paris were absolute bliss, best described as I put it in a Facebook post as "pure, unadulterated happiness."

Later, I suffered the consequences. The day after returning home to the United States, I got an X-ray at the office of a local orthopedic physician. Sticking the X-ray film in a light box, my doctor concluded that I indeed had a stress fracture, pointing to a crack at the top of my left foot. Since I had waited so long to seek treatment, I had to let the broken bone heal itself without the help of a cast or boot. This meant that for the entire month of August after returning from my trip, I was primarily bed- or couch-ridden and unable to participate in any physical activity that required the use of my broken left foot. I fell behind on my daily exercise routine, missed out on hikes with friends, and neglected to experience many of the benefits provided by walking regularly.

And so, I learned an important lesson: In order to walk to change the world, you have to start by taking care of yourself.

When done in moderation, however, walking can be a tool for promoting physical health — from facilitating communication between doctors and patients to improving health outcomes. It's even a tool for fighting a particularly pressing health problem: the global obesity epidemic.

A HEALTH CRISIS OF EPIDEMIC PROPORTIONS

"America Is Fatter Than Ever," reads one infographic from the Centers for Disease Control and Prevention. Nearly 40 percent of adults (aged 20 and older) and 20 percent of youth (aged 2-19) in the United States are obese. This is particularly concerning because obese children and young adults are more likely to remain obese throughout their lives, with 80 percent of overweight children and adolescents growing up to be obese adults. An astounding 70 percent of all Americans are overweight or obese, indicating that Americans with "normal" weight now form a minority.

Contrary to a common misconception, the obesity problem is not limited to high-income countries. According to a study by the Global Obesity Prevention Center, many lower-than-average-income countries including Hungary, Venezuela, and Tunisia have higher-than-average rates of obesity. People of all income levels are susceptible to the risk factors of obesity such as poor diets and low levels of physical activity.

A host of other problems currently threatening the world's health are linked to obesity. Heart disease and stroke, high blood pressure, diabetes, certain cancers, gallbladder disease, osteoarthritis, gout, and respiratory problems such as sleep apnea and asthma, among other issues, all are more likely in individuals who are obese.

PATIENTS AS PARTNERS

In the midst of the global obesity crisis, medical doctor Ted Eytan remains positive.

"It's glass 3/4 full. Always and in all ways," read his personal website and LinkedIn bio. Ted's personal mantra makes it clear that he consistently strives to see the best in others and in the world around him.

His "glass 3/4 full" mentality shines through in his work in public health. Ted (who you met in Step 1) is the Medical Director of the Kaiser Permanente Center for Total Health in Washington, D.C., as well as a physician and family medicine specialist with a focus on preventative health care, total health, and diversity.

While Ted is a Doctor of Medicine, he hesitates to use the title, "Doctor," before his name. He believes that the traditional doctor-patient power dynamic, wherein a health professional makes decisions about the patient's health with little to no input from the patient, is not the most effective mode of treatment. In a doctor's office or hospital, the person in the white coat is typically viewed as the expert and clear default authority figure. This traditional model of care neglects to acknowledge that the patient is the expert on his or her own health.

The study, "Patients as Partners: A Qualitative Study of Patients' Engagement in Their Health Care," argues that patients should have a role as partners in healthcare decisions, especially in the case of chronic illness. The study encourages medical professionals to adopt practices to engage patients in their own health care. In keeping with this study, Ted has found that the opportunity to get to know his patients on a personal level encourages the development of a trusting partnership and permits him to do his job more effectively.

Once, Ted was working with a patient whose condition required a visit to a specialist in a building located down the street from his office.

"I'll walk you there!" Ted said enthusiastically, since the specialist's office was so close.

In the span of only a block, Ted got to know the patient better than he had in the entire time of treating the patient up until that point. His interactions with the patient outside of the traditional medical environment permitted Ted to better understand his patient as a person and gave him unique insight into his patient's condition. The next time Ted treated the patient, he had a better understanding of the patient's experience and could provide more effective personalized care.

Through collaborative experiences such as walking, patients and doctors can build genuine connections and foster understanding in all of their interactions, striving towards a point where a doctor is deeply familiar with a patient's health history and can collaborate with the patient to prevent potential health problems.

"When you walk with someone, you are going somewhere with them as opposed to for them," Ted says.

For this reason, he believes walking is a particularly effective way to encourage partnership between doctors and patients. In this case, the simple act of going for a walk together transformed the doctor-patient relationship from one of hierarchy to one of collaborative care.

TOTAL HEALTH

Growing up, I was deeply perplexed by the sheer quantity of different medical providers that my parents visited. There were cardiologists, primary care physicians, physical therapists, gastroenterologists, chiropractors, and other big words that I couldn't pronounce at the time. My brother and I would often get dragged along to a variety of these healthcare appointments, patiently entertaining ourselves in the waiting rooms and trying to figure out — often without success — what exactly each doctor did.

The different aspects of medical care — whether it's cardiology, neurology, sports medicine, or any of a number of other medical disciplines — are often fragmented, with specialists in each field who are separately responsible for different parts of patient health. The Kaiser Permanente Center for Total Health, where Ted has been the medical director since it opened in

2011, serves to close these gaps. It's focused on promoting "total health" by further developing relationships not only between doctors and patients but also among policymakers and the health sector. According to the Center's website, "[it's] a place for innovators, leaders, influencers, thinkers, and believers in wellness to talk about health." Essentially, the Center for Total Health is a health innovation center, facilitating important conversations about the future of health.

Always intrigued by any mention of "innovation," I was interested to learn more about Kaiser Permanente's work to improve outcomes for patients. Kaiser Permanente is a non-profit health plan that serves approximately 12 million people. With Kaiser Permanente, a patient pays for health plans and insurance upfront instead of paying after care is given. Furthermore, doctors are not paid based on the care they give when a patient is sick or the quantity of medications they prescribe to patients. Instead, a portion of their compensation is linked to quality of care (measured by certain desirable health outcomes) and service (measured by patient satisfaction). Doctors are also incentivized to reduce medical costs in order to increase their compensation. In this way, Kaiser Permanente is uniquely incentivized to improve patient health because its business model stipulates that it does better when patients are healthier.

"Our business model is really simple. People get sick, we lose money," Ted says. As a result, Kaiser Permanente offers a unique focus on health and wellness along with its more traditional role of treating medical problems as they occur.

In keeping with this mission, Kaiser Permanente promotes active lifestyles to improve total patient health, which it defines as including physical, mental, and social well-being. One of the ways Kaiser Permanente does this is by simply encouraging patients to go for a walk.

WALKING AWAY THE HEALTH PROBLEMS

"Walking is a simple way to make a big change in your health," according to Dr. Bob Sallis, a family physician at Kaiser Permanente Fontana Medical Center. Dr. Sallis believes that walking is a "wonder drug" capable of remedying many of today's most pervasive medical problems. From diabetes, depression, breast and colon cancer, and high blood pressure, to cardiovascular disease, obesity, anxiety, and osteoporosis, all of these medical conditions can be cured, prevented, or reduced in severity through just 30 minutes of walking per day five days a week, according to the Center for Total Health. Walking is a particularly effective treatment because — unlike many other forms of exercise — it's low-impact and doesn't require an investment in equipment or a gym membership.

As a testament to the power of walking, Dr. Sallis has witnessed patients with diabetes who have seen their diabetes go away after beginning a walking program. While type 2 diabetes alone currently accounts for 34 percent of all Medicare costs, walking provides a free method of treatment and prevention. Unlike most prescription medications, the benefits of walking are almost immediate. According to Dr. Sallis, walking is a free medication with a host of other health benefits that other prescription medications cannot claim.

George Halvorson, the former Chairman and CEO of Kaiser Permanente, echoes these sentiments, arguing that the only way to overcome the chronic disease epidemics currently facing the world is through walking. Making walking a daily habit has wide-ranging health benefits, from reducing the likelihood of stroke in women by 43 percent to shortening the symptom time for the common cold by 46 percent.

"There's no guarantee that doing any particular thing will work for any given person," Halvorson recognizes. Still, in the face of the laundry list of positive health outcomes associated with walking, he argues that, "it's pretty hard for anyone who cares about their own health not to look very hard at how walking can become a major part of what we do."

Through its focus on long-term patient well-being and its emphasis on preventative care mechanisms such as walking, Kaiser Permanente has gained recognition as the number one national and regional provider in key areas from Consumer Reports, J.D. Power, Medicare, National Committee for Quality Assurance (NCQA), and other rating organizations.

The principles of "total health" are gaining momentum outside of the Kaiser Permanente health system. The two most recent United States Surgeons General, Dr. Regina Benjamin and Dr. Vivek Murthy, are strong proponents of walking and walkability. The work of both Surgeons General, beginning with Benjamin's appointment by President Barack Obama in 2009, led to the issuance of a formal Call to Action on Walking in the United States.

"A 30-minute walk is better than any pill," believes Benjamin, an advocate of preventative medicine.

In keeping with this unique model of preventative care, the Surgeons General encourage doctors to check patients' physical activity levels — especially time spent walking — in addition to routine health metrics such as blood pressure.

"Walking is an easy and inexpensive way to improve the health and well-being of all Americans," asserts the Office of the Surgeon General. "Now is the time to step it up and make walking a national priority."

A STEP IN THE RIGHT DIRECTION

Regardless of how much he told his patients about the overwhelming benefits of walking, Dr. David Sabgir was frustrated that he could not get his patients to change their behavior. Dr. Sabgir, a cardiologist based out of Columbus, Ohio, knows a thing or two about the health benefits of walking.

"There are over 40 diseases that walking either prevents or treats," he marvels.

When he isn't with patients, he spends most of the day walking at his treadmill desk or walking around the medical care facility where he works, taking in all of the health benefits of the simple form of exercise. On the weekends, he can be found taking long walks around his local park.

One spring Saturday morning, he decided to invite his patients to join him for a walk in the park where he typically spends his weekends. He was overwhelmed by the response, as more than one hundred people joined him. This successful experiment led Dr. Sabgir to formalize the practice through Walk with a Doc.

Founded in 2005, Walk with a Doc began as a grassroots movement in which doctors would give a brief presentation on a health topic and then lead participants on a walk. Now, Walk with a Doc offers a formalized program that can easily be put into action by doctors. The organization has expanded to more than 300 cities around the world.

The Walk with a Doc website is filled with the stories of walkers and doctors who have been personally impacted by the organization's work. Steve Sharp, from Dallas, Texas, was an active high school athlete who gained weight after 40 years of smoking and reducing his levels of physical activity. His increasingly large belly became a "pain in the you know what."

After just one year of participating in Walk with a Doc, Steve lost 20 pounds. Walking became an integral part of his daily routine, and it led him to embrace other forms of physical activity such as biking. He has developed personal relationships with the doctor who leads his walks, Dr. Helfand, as well as the fellow walkers who hold him accountable to his wellness goals. After Steve had a carotid subclavian bypass surgery, Dr. Helfand visited him in the hospital, a testament to the strength of the patient-doctor relationships fostered by Walk with a Doc.

"Walking has motivated me to change my life, and other parts of my health as well," Steve says, attesting to the power of walking in turning his life around.

A GATEWAY DRUG

"Walking is the great hope. It's the gateway drug," asserts Tom Richards.

Tom, the Director of Community Engagement at the American Council on Exercise (ACE), believes that getting people to start — and continue — walking is the key to opening the door to a broader spectrum of physical activity. ACE's goal is to put people on the road to a more active and fulfilling life through physical activity of any kind — in short, "to get people moving." To achieve this mission, ACE facilitates partnerships with fitness industry professionals, policymakers, community organizations, and the healthcare industry as a whole.

Tom first became interested in health and healthcare policy because he wanted to help affordably distribute healthcare goods. Early on in his career, Tom recognized that physical activity was an under-utilized treatment method and a potential asset in achieving this mission. Exercise, he believed, could be a useful tool in making healthcare more affordable. Prior to joining ACE, Tom was the President of the National Coalition for Promoting Physical Activity, which fosters collaborative partnerships between public, private, and industry efforts in order to inspire and empower people to be more physically active. In his position at ACE, Tom promotes prescribing physical activity as treatment for inactivity-related health problems.

"'Exercise is good for you,' is not a controversial statement," Tom asserts.

In this way, ACE's goal to get people moving sounds easy enough. However, individuals get caught up in questions of what is the right amount or type of exercise. They don't know where to start, so they don't start at all. They get wrapped up in busy schedules, claim not to like exercise, can't afford gym memberships or class subscriptions, struggle to commit to exercise routines, or find it painful, among other excuses.

In response to each of these excuses, Tom has one recommendation: Walk.

Tom believes that walking is a particularly accessible way to get people moving because it is so easy to do. While time is a common obstacle to someone starting an exercise regime of any kind, the beauty of walking is that the timing is completely at the discretion of the individual. It can even be integrated into daily life. Walking doesn't require a monetary investment, and it permits individuals at any fitness level to pace themselves and gradually build up endurance. Tom acknowledges that, while there are many reasons people have for not exercising, there are very few people who dislike walking.

"No one regrets a 10-minute walk," Tom believes. After going for a walk of any length, Tom notices that his heart is pumping, his legs feel stronger, and everything seems to just work better.

Unlike some of the other health epidemics facing society, inactivity can't be cured by any vaccine. Regardless of the infrastructure or other measures that are put into place to encourage walking, Tom believes that people ultimately will not walk unless they are motivated and encouraged. For this reason, he believes that efforts to create supportive work, home, and community environments — such as Walk with a Doc — are particularly effective at encouraging people to start and continue routines of walking or any other form of physical activity.

While he does recognize the positive strides made by exercise technology such as activity trackers, Tom still worries that technology will add fuel to the fire of the inactivity epidemic. Technology affords the opportunity to achieve high levels of productivity without moving. As a result, experiencing the benefits of walking necessitates a degree of intentionality. When it comes to increasing physical activity, everyone — even the most dedicated bodybuilder — can use a bit of encouragement.

"If you're not going to walk for yourself, walk for other people or ask other people to go for a walk," Tom advises. "It's a compassionate thing to do."

Aside from the individual benefits, walking and its associated health outcomes promote positive effects to be shared among all members of society. For instance, implementing walking as a plan for prevention and treatment of diabetes would result in enough cost savings to allow programs such as Medicare in the United States to be sustainable for the future.

As Ted likes to say, "Health is about who you inhabit the world with."

Being healthy means knowing your neighbors, contributing to the community, and being well in all senses of the word. What better way to start on the path towards total health than by walking?

———

In the same way that a team is only as good as its weakest player, society is only as good as its least healthy individuals. If those individuals are walking towards better health, then all of society will benefit as a result.

STEP 3.

MENTAL WELLBEING

———

"If there were a pill that people could take that would… reduce the risk of cognitive decline and depression, reduce stress, and improve emotional wellbeing, everyone would be clamoring to take it, it would be flying off the shelves," says Dr. JoAnn Manson, a Professor of Epidemiology at Harvard's School of Public Health. "But that pill really is available to everyone in the form of 30 minutes a day of brisk walking."

Worldwide, over one billion people suffer from mental or substance abuse disorders. In the United States alone, approximately 61.5 million people — or one in five adults — experience mental illness in a given year.

The consequences of mental health conditions on society are staggering. According to *The American Journal of Psychiatry*,

"Serious mental illness costs America $193.2 billion in lost earnings per year." People with mental health conditions have the highest education dropout rate of any disability group and face an increased risk of chronic medical conditions.

Suicide is the leading cause of death in the United States for people aged 15 to 24. Among those children who die by suicide, 90 percent have a mental health condition. This macabre fact shows that the wellness of society starts with mental wellbeing.

Although it touches nearly every aspect of society, mental health is often stigmatized and not given the public attention it deserves. In 2015, only 40 percent of those in the United States with mental health conditions received treatment, meaning that the majority of mental health conditions went untreated.

Walking could be the pill to improve mental wellbeing.

BEST FOOT FORWARD

"Why is walking a particularly effective way of improving mental health?" I ask, knowing that Professor of Sociology Sarah Stiles will undoubtedly have a bit of wisdom to share.

Sitting in her tidy Georgetown University office overlooking the Potomac River on a blue-skied spring day, Professor Stiles is enlightening me on the merits of walking for mental wellbeing. Our conversation itself feels like a meditative experience, as the room is filled with the sounds of Professor Stiles' calm voice and birds chirping outside the open window, and the walls are adorned with posters promoting mindfulness and wellness.

The sound of an airplane flying overhead interrupts the peace.

"What walks on four legs in the morning, two legs in the afternoon, three legs in the evening, and no legs at night?" Professor Stiles asks in return, citing Greek mythology's Riddle of the Sphinx.

I've heard this riddle before, but this was not quite the response I anticipated. "A human during childhood, adulthood, old age, and death," I answer tentatively, unsure of how this relates to my question.

"Exactly. Walking is something common to the human race. We all walk," Professor Stiles states simply.

＊ ＊ ＊

As a critical part of the human experience, Professor Stiles believes that walking is a natural and necessary component of human flourishing.

"Mental health is linked to flourishing as individuals and as a community," she asserts. "If we want to make a positive impact in our communities, we have to be at peak performance."

Professor Stiles, who has encountered mental illness among her family, friends, and students, speaks from experience. Both of Professor Stiles' parents were clinically depressed and were never treated. While attending law school at Northeastern University, Professor Stiles' own mental health problems came to a head. She didn't know how to cope with the stress brought on by her coursework, or with the resultant mental health problems. Stress was keeping her from flourishing in and out of the classroom.

Professor Stiles recognized that the "toxic stress" was negatively impacting her health, sleep, and performance. She was forced to face her mental illness head-on.

"Life can't be misery all of the time," she thought desperately one day when her workload was feeling particularly burdensome.

Her friend Wendy, a Tibetan Buddhist, suggested that she try meditating.

I don't have time to meditate, was the first thought that entered Professor Stiles' mind.

Her friend suggested that she give walking meditation a try.

To Professor Stiles, it seemed like the perfect compromise.

I can get somewhere and meditate at the same time, she thought. Later, she learned that this was not really the idea behind walking meditation.

Professor Stiles started listening to John Kabat-Zinn's "Guided Mindfulness Meditation Series" while walking throughout her typical daily routine. Meditation changed Professor Stiles' life, lifting the weight of her stress and the baggage she had been carrying for far too long. Walking meditation proved to be Professor Stiles' entry point into other styles of meditation.

"When we meditate and are mindful, we realize that there is no other moment than this moment," she says. Meditation permits her to recognize that dwelling in the past and worrying about the future are both a waste of time.

Through meditation, Professor Stiles is completely present in each moment. Free from external influences, she can access her pure core beneath layers of socialization. With this clarity of mind, Professor Stiles can better understand her mission and purpose.

According to Professor Stiles, meditation of any kind enhances your ability to change the world. Walking meditation is particularly impactful because of the self-awareness it permits.

"Notice that you are picking up the foot ... and then coming down on the heel ..." Professor Stiles says in a soft, slow voice, simulating what it's like to do walking meditation. "Feel that the pressure comes back on the ball of the foot ... as the other leg swings forward ..."

While walking meditation can be done anywhere — in this case, in Professor Stiles' shoebox of an office — Professor Stiles believes that the ideal circumstance for walking meditation is a quiet place in order to limit distractions. A labyrinth, a circle in which the meditator walks through a maze-like pattern to arrive at the center, provides an ideal setting to relax the mind.

"There is so much going on that we really are oblivious to," Professor Stiles recognizes, marveling at the power of the body. Not everyone takes the time to relate to the body in this nuanced way.

When I leave Professor Stiles' office at the conclusion of our conversation, I take the time to think about each of my footsteps. While I often walk around Georgetown's campus with my head in my phone or my mind going through a mental list of tasks to accomplish, I take this time on my walk back to my house to attempt mindful walking.

The stress that I was feeling about completing the day's list of tasks begins to dissipate as I direct my attention towards my feet rather than my own thoughts. I feel more conscious of my posture, making an effort to stand up straight under the heavy load of my full backpack. I am increasingly aware of my breathing, and I try to breathe more deeply than my typical shallow inhales and exhales.

I notice so much more about my surroundings during my walk: the sound of people laughing on the front lawn, the breeze on my face, the puffy clouds crawling slowly through the sky, the smell of some unnamed meat wafting through the air from the dining hall. When I am distracted by my phone or my thoughts, so much of this goes unnoticed. But when I am walking consciously, I can feel myself become more present and calm in the short 10-minute walk home.

It is this precise attention to the body's health and wellbeing, Professor Stiles believes, that permits an individual to change the world.

OVERWORKED + UNDERWALKED

In her role as an educator, Professor Stiles recognizes that mental health conditions are particularly prevalent on college campuses. In 2014, 30 percent of college students "reported feeling depressed to the point where it negatively impacted their ability to function." A staggering 7.5 percent of college students reported having seriously considered suicide in the past 12 months.

In the fall of 2017, I took Professor Stiles' class "Social Entrepreneurship: Leading Social Change." In this course, we learned to be social entrepreneurs and to "think creatively, act ethically, and empower others to do the same." A critical component of our coursework was a focus on wellness.

"Social entrepreneurship is a lifestyle of wellness," Professor Stiles teaches her students. "If we are to solve or at least ameliorate the apparently intractable social issues we face, we need to be at our best. Oftentimes we compromise our health and general wellness in order to 'get things done.' The irony is that we are actually less effective when we are compromised than when we are thriving."

I learned from Professor Stiles that in order to make a positive impact in our communities we have to be at peak performance.

In college and in the working world, I've found that there is a stigma against taking breaks. There's a prevalent idea that breaks of any kind — whether it is sleep or exercise or any other period of inactivity — are not productive or are a sign of weakness.

"If time is money, then breaks look like a waste of time, and that's a waste of money," Professor Stiles says about the toxic culture of the working world. In reality, breaks—especially ones that involve walking—can help improve mental functioning and performance.

I've experienced the transformative impact of walking breaks firsthand.

During finals season in the second semester of my senior year of college, I had an overwhelming number of writing assignments. Deadlines were soon approaching, and I had posted up at my desk in my second-story bedroom of my Georgetown townhouse, opening the windows in hopes of breathing in some inspiration.

After a few hours of writing nonstop, I hit a wall. My vision was beginning to blur after staring at my computer screen for so long. I tried to type, but the words had stopped flowing. I couldn't write a coherent sentence to save my life.

Keep pushing through, I thought, hoping inspiration would strike sooner or later. I went downstairs to get a snack, wishing it would fuel my brain, but after another hour of sitting at my desk, I had only a few subpar sentences to show for it.

"S.O.S. I'm going stir crazy. Anyone want to take a walking

break?" I texted my friends, all of whom were also in the middle of finals.

This is a bad idea. I don't have time for a break, I thought immediately after sending the text, knowing that my deadlines were quickly approaching.

Abby and Caroline responded, and we decided to meet up a few minutes later. As we walked and talked, I could feel my mind begin to relax for the first time all day. Breathing in the fresh air, I noticed the stiffness in my legs and back go away as we walked to the Georgetown Waterfront.

On our way back towards home, the ideas started flowing. I tried to take notes on my phone, but the inspiration was hitting faster than I could type.

As soon as I got back to my house, I cranked out the last bit of what I needed to write for one assignment and moved on to the next. After writing more effectively in an hour than I had all day, I opened my phone to see messages from Abby and Caroline.

"So glad we did that. I just cranked out so much of my paper," Abby had texted.

"Couldn't agree more," Caroline concurred.

While taking a walking break initially seemed like a waste of time, it turned out to be the most efficient way to spend my time, boosting my mental performance and personal satisfaction.

Science agrees.

When you're doing goal-oriented work that requires concentration or logical thinking — indeed, most "work" falls into these categories — the prefrontal cortex is working hard. A study from the University of Illinois shows that, when faced with a long task, imposing brief breaks on yourself will improve your long-term focus on the task. The benefits I experienced through my hour-long walk can indeed be realized through just a five-minute walking break once per hour of work.

"Standing up and walking around for five minutes every hour during the workday could lift your mood, combat lethargy without reducing focus and attention, and even dull hunger pangs," a study of desk workers concluded.

While it is well-known that sleep is essential for consolidating memories and improving brain function, scientists have also found that taking walking breaks simulates similar memory consolidation and improved learning.

"Downtime replenishes the brain's stores of attention and motivation, encourages productivity and creativity, and is essential to both achieve our highest levels of performance and simply form stable memories in everyday life," science writer Ferris Jabr confirms. "Moments of respite may even be necessary to keep one's moral compass in working order and maintain a sense of self."

The evidence in favor of walking breaks is stacked high. Allowing more people to realize the benefits of these breaks, however, will be a matter of changing workplace culture and societal norms around productivity, which you'll learn more about in Step 9.

Even when your mental health is in tip-top shape, walking provides the mental break required to reach peak performance. When it comes to difficult times — when your mental health is comprised — these breaks are even more essential. Walking provides the literal change of pace required for healing during such moments of pain.

WALKING AWAY THE PAIN

"It's important to live slowly through moments of pain," Nina Lund-Simon reflects.

When Nina, a recent Georgetown University graduate, was studying abroad during her junior year of college in Denmark, one of her friends died suddenly in a tragic boating accident at the Copenhagen Harbor.

Coping with death is one of the more difficult aspects of life. Coping with death in the context of a study abroad experience — when you are away from home in a foreign country during what is supposed to be a carefree, joy-filled period — is unimaginable.

Nina went through the motions of her last few weeks in Copenhagen, finishing up her exams and counting down the days until she could leave the place where the tragedy had occurred. However, it would be a few more weeks before she could return home to Washington, D.C. She had already scheduled a non-refundable solo backpacking trip to her home country of France.

"I was forced to have two weeks in France by myself with my emotions," Nina recalls. "And it's the healthiest thing that has ever happened to me."

Walking alone through the cities of France, Nina had to confront her grief head-on. Surrounded by the beauty of each city she visited, Nina experienced a slower pace of life and took the time required to endure each stage of the grieving process. While there were moments when she acutely felt the pain of her loss, Nina found an overarching sense of peace and long-term healing by the end of her trip.

"When you're forced to have moments of complete loneliness, you start to see the beauty in that loneliness and to see that as an opportunity for self-reflection and growth," she attests. "And that's fruitful for the rest of your life."

This experience contrasts with another period of grief that Nina experienced in high school. After the death of one of her high school friends, Nina coped by turning to strenuous exercise. Compressing her emotions, Nina worked out whenever she had a spare moment and tried to avoid having to face the reality of the death of her friend.

"I was too active and because of that I never completely healed from it," she reflects. "I think by having that opportunity to really delve into each aspect of pain, that's the only way that you can truly heal long-term."

WALK IT OUT

Walking by herself proved to be the best way for Nina to cope with her grief. Unlike other forms of exercise, walking is a relatively monotonous, low-impact form of physical exertion. For these reasons, it is linked to some serious mental health benefits.

While the connection between walking and improved mental health is well-documented, there's still research to be done about the exact scientific relationship between walking and mental wellbeing. According to researchers at New Mexico Highlands University, the foot's impact during walking results in increased blood flow in the brain. This increased blood flow leads to a greater degree of brain function and an enhanced sense of wellbeing. Although the foot's impact is lower when walking than when running, walking is associated with a greater degree of blood flow to the brain than running is, for reasons not yet scientifically understood.

Along with providing her with space to grieve, Nina has found that walking has improved other aspects of her mental health.

When Nina was in middle school, she lived in Spain for a year. She didn't speak the language and, as a result, did not have a lot of friends. This deep sense of loneliness posed a threat to Nina's mental health. Instead, Nina's time in Spain became a period of growth, which she credits to her time spent walking.

Each day, she walked one hour to and from school. Popping in her headphones, she would play her favorite songs on a loop during her walk. Nina began to cherish the feeling of being completely and utterly alone, as she had the chance to be by herself with her thoughts and to manipulate her environment through her musical choices.

"When you're in extremely different environments with

different languages and different ways of living, it's important to have this moment of self-reflection and to just understand the essence of being you," Nina attests. "And I think walking achieves that."

Nina has lived in France, Costa Rica, Spain, Los Angeles, Denmark, and Washington, D.C., among others, and she's traveled to countless other places around the globe. In the face of the relative instability of her frequent changes in geographical location, walking remains a constant in her life. Regardless of how the context of her physical location changes, the act of walking is essentially the same wherever she is in the world. For Nina, walking is a source of comfort, stability, and inspiration.

"Most situations in life are completely out of your control," Nina elaborates. "But I do think that walking completely changes that. It's your opportunity to manipulate — at least to some extent — the outcome of the situation. It gives time to set your body, change your posture, and get into both the physical and mental mindset necessary for a situation."

Whenever she needs to prepare for an interview, an exam, or an important conversation, Nina first goes for a walk. As a neuroscience major, she knows just how beneficial those steps can be for achieving peak mental performance.

Walking's connection to improving memory and boosting brain power can best be explained by a phenomenon known as transient hypofrontality. In layman's terms, transient hypofrontality means that walking temporarily decreases activity in certain parts of the brain, particularly the frontal lobes which are responsible for memory, judgement, and language. As a result, the brain adopts a different style of thinking that can lead to improved creativity and productivity.

On top of those benefits, cardiovascular exercise of any kind is associated with the generation of new brain cells and the creation of brain-derived protein which helps with decision-making, thinking, and learning.

When it comes to the daunting task of writing an academic paper, Nina relies on walking as an essential part of her writing process. Rather than the traditional ritual of sitting down in front of a computer and waiting for inspiration to strike, Nina goes out for a long walk to consolidate her thoughts. Then, once she has essentially written the paper in her head, she types out the words of her paper in a comparatively short amount of time.

"People have a tendency to sit in front of a laptop and choose a thesis and start writing," Nina explains. "And that directs your paper in a way that completely suppresses the opportunity for range. If you allow yourself to think without direction, then you achieve direction by attaining places you would not have thought of before."

And if her endeavors don't go exactly as planned, Nina walks to cope with the results.

"Whenever I go through a breakup or failing an exam or getting rejected from a job, the first thought is: how do I consolidate those thoughts and feelings in a healthy way?" Nina says. "And the only way I do that is by popping in my headphones and going for a walk."

Nina credits her countless walks throughout her life with who she is today. From reflecting while walking alone to engaging in deep conversations while walking with friends, Nina has reaped the benefits of reduced stress and anxiety, improved memory, human connection, and increased creativity and productivity.

A WALK IN THE PARK

As Nina discovered through her outdoor walks, the mental health benefits of walking are especially acute in green spaces. Two studies in particular demonstrate the positive impact associated with walking in rural settings.

The first one was conducted by Dr. Jenny Roe, an environmental psychologist committed to designing places that improve health and social outcomes for people. Her research found that exposure to nature leads to greater productivity and decreased stress. Now, she is dedicated to improving access to nature for vulnerable groups so that a greater number of people can partake in these benefits.

In the study, Dr. Roe and her colleagues at Heriot-Watt University in the United Kingdom were determined to find an objective measure for the emotional benefits of walking. They used mobile brain wave scans to study brain activity as volunteers walked for about 1.5 miles through both urban and rural spaces in Edinburgh, Scotland. Volunteers started walking through a moderately busy historic shopping district, proceeded to a path in a park, and finished in a heavily trafficked commercial district, with an equal distance of 0.5 miles allotted to each phase of the course for a total time of about half an hour.

When the volunteers were walking through the urban parts of the course, their brain wave patterns demonstrated that they were more mentally frustrated compared to when walking through the park. On the other hand, when walking through green spaces, they reached a state that mimicked the brain's status during meditation. Despite reaching a more meditative state, the volunteers were not zoned out. They were still engaged in their environment but in a more effortless way, free from the many distractions of busy city streets.

"It's called involuntary attention in psychology," Dr. Roe told *The New York Times* in an interview. "It holds our attention while at the same time allowing scope for reflection."

This study reinforces the role of walking, especially in green spaces, in promoting mental recovery and encouraging peak mental performance.

The second study was conducted by Dr. Gregory Bratman and his colleagues at Stanford University. Through their study of the impact of natural experience on cognitive function and mental health, the researchers found that walking in nature decreases anxiety and improves cognition.

The researchers evaluated the affective and cognitive functioning of 60 study participants both before and after they went on a 50-minute walk in either a natural or urban environment in Stanford, California. Those who participated in the nature walk experienced less anxiety, greater positive affect, and enhanced working memory performance compared to those who completed the urban walk. The nature walkers also experienced a lower degree of rumination, defined by Dr. Bratman as "a focus on the negative aspects of oneself in a repetitive way." Notably, rumination is associated with a negative mood and is a risk factor for depression.

At the end of the day, regardless of the setting, walking is beneficial for mental health. As these studies show, green space can amplify the mental health benefits of walking.

The reality facing our world, however, is that access to green space is unequal, a phenomenon that will be exaggerated in the future if there are not more efforts to increase access to green space. With growing rates of urbanization and more than 50 percent of people already living in cities, it is important not only to focus on preserving nature outside of cities but also to bring nature into cities, Dr. Bratman believes. If we can't allow everyone to experience nature in its purest form, then we at least need to simulate that experience in cities in a way that is broadly accessible.

Dr. Roe believes that poor communities, which would benefit most from green space, are those that currently have the least access. While wealthier individuals often experience a good kind of stress related to goal attainment, according to the Brookings Institution, poor individuals typically encounter a bad kind of stress "associated with struggling to cope." Dr. Roe has dedicated her career to improving the equality of landscape design in poor urban communities, quantifying the mental health benefits of green space in order to lobby for increased funding.

In order for access to green space to be truly equitable, it must gain traction as being an issue of public health, rather than one of pure aesthetics. According to Dr. Roe, collaboration between a city's public health and urban planning departments is required to increase access to green space and the mental health benefits it provides.

Walk21 founder Jim Walker reduces it to a question of happiness. After all, exercise releases endorphins, which create feelings of happiness and can alleviate the symptoms of people who are anxious or clinically depressed.

"Do you want your people to be happy?" he asks politicians simply.

If the answer is truly "yes," this commitment will be reflected in all of a city's public spending decisions.

———

Backed by a combination of personal experiences and scientific evidence, walking is the avenue to a mentally healthier society. Not only are mentally healthy people better for society, but also there's a clear connection between being mentally well and making an impact. As Professor Stiles says, "We make social impact when we are at our best. When we know ourselves, then we can know others. And only then, when we've been in their shoes, can we achieve lasting impact."

PHASE II

STRENGTH IN NUMBERS

STEP 4.

EMPATHY + UNDERSTANDING

———

"I was taught to hate Palestinians."

As an Israeli citizen, Osnat Ita Skoblinski grew up under the impression that all Arabs were evil. As a child, she lived through the first Gulf War, suicide bombings in Tel Aviv, and the Second Intifada (the second Palestinian uprising against Israel). During this period, she was taught to take two things for granted: 1) "Arabs are bad" and 2) "Israel's army is the most moral in the world."

While out for a walk during a family trip to the United States after high school, Osnat had a chance encounter with a Palestinian man. He was the same age as her, with mutual friends and similar interests. They became fast friends, and he shared with her the Palestinian perspective of the conflict.

"It must be propaganda," she thought. She struggled to believe that her country could be anything other than unquestionably right.

Challenging her biases was a long road of introspection, discussion and controversy with family and friends, as well as sifting through information with a critical lens to determine what to believe. Now, she is an activist promoting a peaceful end to the Israel-Palestine conflict. It was a gradual process, with four years in between meeting her Palestinian friend and beginning her activism work.

All of this — the series of events that quite literally changed the trajectory of her life — occurred as a result of encountering an individual with an experience different from her own.

"We must continue to engage in dialogue with people who disagree with us, or see us as enemies from within," Osnat shares. "Only by meeting other people, only through discourse and understanding — and, of course, by exposure to information — can the world begin to change."

* * *

In October 2017, more than 30,000 Israeli and Palestinian women joined together to walk hand-in-hand for peace, moving through the West Bank and Israel to their final destination of Jerusalem. The march organizer, Women Wage Peace, was founded with the goal of promoting lasting peace in a region of the world that has come to accept conflict as the norm.

"Among us are women from right-wing parties, left-wing parties, Jews and Arabs, women from cities and rural areas. Together we have decided to prevent the next war," says Marilyn Smadja, one of the Women Wage Peace founders. By walking peacefully together, the women not only communicate their demands for a peaceful end to the Israel-Palestine conflict but also visibly demonstrate that peace between Israel and Palestine is attainable.

The unrest between Israel and Palestine is just one of the ongoing conflicts currently facing the world. From religious conflicts and civil wars to nuclear wars and terrorist attacks, the resolution of these clashes lies beyond the capabilities of any one person. Encounters such as Osnat's will not single-handedly end the conflict that engulfs the world.

But walking does facilitate interactions that change hearts and minds on a small scale. And all together, these mindset shifts have the power to promote a more peaceful and understanding world.

A TALE OF TWO CITIES

"Washington is known to be deeply divided—not just between warring Democrats and Republicans but also between the relatively affluent and diverse city west of the Anacostia River and the largely black and long-neglected one east of it."

In *The Economist's* "Tour of a Changing Capital," the unnamed author and two companions explore the inequality that exists in the nation's capital through the lens of walking. Within the city, the 20.7 percent unemployment rate to the east of the Anacostia River is notably more than three times the 6.6 percent unemployment rate to the west of the Anacostia. It is possible for someone living west of the Anacostia to rarely cross to the other side of the river, and vice versa, further reinforcing existing inequalities.

The article, written in January 2017, proposes that spending a day strolling through the city is the best way to learn about how the city is evolving. Walking 17 zigzagged miles from one end of the city to the other, the author begins his journey in the Anacostia neighborhood in Southeast D.C.

Traveling through the neighborhood by foot, the author and his friends are surprised to notice that the neighborhood to the east of the Anacostia River is so "pleasant and peaceful." They stroll past Civil War defenses overlooking the city and the Potomac River, and they see colonial homes, neighborhood churches, and libraries. The longer they walk, however, the more they notice the lack of something essential: food sources.

In sections of the more affluent Northwest quadrant of D.C., it isn't uncommon to find multiple grocery stores in the span of a block. In contrast, the section of D.C. to the east of the Anacostia is formally classified as a "food desert," with only three supermarkets serving the more than 140,000 people who live in Wards 7 and 8.

The author and his friends continue their walk, passing massive new developments, government buildings, museums, and monuments to the country's past, concluding their journey in Northwest Washington.

The final paragraphs of the reflection are the most telling:

"In some respects, the contrast between the morning walk and the last stretch couldn't be greater. Most of the faces are now white. Instead of a food desert, there is a cornucopia of Safeways, Giants, and Whole Foods Markets...

"Moreover, unlike Anacostia, where change is in the air, this part of north-west Washington seems almost exactly as your correspondent left it 20 years ago. The flower store is still there. Our old house on Van Ness Street, a picture-book red brick colonial, is just the same as ever—except, of course, for its value, which according to Zillow, an online property database, has risen more than threefold since we left it.

"And yet in another respect these two ends of town are remarkably similar—and that is the final surprise of this walk across Washington. The houses in the two neighbourhoods look interchangeable. The landscaping is the same. The evening tranquility in the north-west, amid the greenery and the birdsong, feels much like the morning peace in the south-east. It's seven o'clock and getting dark at the yellow-bordered sign on Massachusetts Avenue saying 'Maryland welcomes you,' and it feels almost as if the walk has come full circle."

When the people who live to the west and east of the Anacostia River rarely interact, it reinforces the differences that set them apart. As I've learned from my own experiences, walking has the power to bridge divides, allowing people to better understand each other's lived experiences and to find that they are more similar than they might have imagined.

✳ ✳ ✳

Living for four years on Georgetown's campus in Northwest D.C., I rarely ventured into any of the city's other quadrants, especially parts of the city east of the Anacostia River. An internship during the fall semester of my senior year, however, required two of my classmates and I to travel into Southeast D.C. on a biweekly basis.

The internship was with the National Reentry Network for Returning Citizens, an organization that helps previously incarcerated individuals become contributing members of society. Friends warned us to be on high alert when entering this part of town, which has a reputation for being unsafe for three unaccompanied white women, especially after dark. Driving into Anacostia, we noticed a departure from the grand halls of democracy to the west of the river. In our car, we caught glimpses of row homes, schools, gas stations, and recreational centers, all lacking the imposing grandeur of the structures to the west of the river.

During the final weeks of our internship, we had the chance to walk through the streets of Southeast D.C. with Courtney Stewart, Chairman and CEO of the National Reentry Network. Courtney — clearly admired in the community — smiled and waved at everyone we passed on the neighborhood's streets. In the community, we had the chance to stop and talk to returning citizens, learning about their experiences and the challenges of reentering society after being in prison.

While we had been warned to fear for our safety, I felt perfectly at ease in the neighborhood, experiencing it as a community member with Courtney as our guide. During our internship we had become accustomed to driving across the city, parking directly in front of the Reentry Network office, doing our work, and getting back in the car to drive back to school, without spending any time in the neighborhood where we worked.

Had we not taken the time to experience the neighborhood by walking in it, we would have missed this opportunity to learn from the community members themselves and to better understand their needs. At the conclusion of the internship, I wished there were more opportunities for residents of the divided city of Washington to reverse their preconceived notions about their neighbors on the other side of the river.

＊ ＊ ＊

The 11th Street Bridge Park, expected to open in late 2019, was designed with the explicit purpose of connecting the inhabitants on both sides of the Anacostia River. With the goal of bridging the gaps between the inhabitants on both sides of the river, the park is anticipated to be Washington, D.C's first elevated public park. In a way reminiscent of New York City's famous High Line, the park makes use of the pillars from a cross-river road bridge that had fallen into disrepair.

"It will be a destination — more a place than a path," according to project director Scott Kratz.

The act of two groups of people being physically present together in a space is essential for understanding. In this tale of two cities, the people to the east and west of the Anacostia River rarely interact, which means that there are limited opportunities for either group to understand the other's experience. In a scenario of limited interaction, it is easy to rely on stereotypes about the people who inhabit the other side of the river, without taking the time to evaluate the truth behind the stereotypes. While this one park cannot be expected to single-handedly unite the two Washingtons, it offers an important entry point for bridging the gap in other ways in the future.

The project's team is particularly conscious of the gentrification that occurred in the Chelsea neighborhood in the aftermath of the construction of the High Line, which you'll learn about in more detail in Step 8. Mr. Kratz has developed an "Equitable Development Plan," in order to encourage the development of small businesses and to create a homebuyers' club for locals to capture any economic benefits of the park. With its attention to benefit-sharing, this project is clearly being undertaken with the best interest of the community at heart.

While the Anacostia River has historically divided Washington, the 11st Street Bridge Park will bring together people who wouldn't normally interact. These kinds of simple interactions in a shared place are the first step in facilitating understanding among people from different backgrounds. Changing hearts and minds, however, requires stepping out of your comfort zone.

EXPERIENCING HOMELESSNESS

A walk to the grocery store. That's all it took to entirely transform my perspective on homelessness.

Every Sunday morning during my junior year at Georgetown University, I would walk from my on-campus apartment, down M Street, and to the Trader Joe's near the Foggy Bottom Metro Station. Each week, I noticed that I would walk past the same individuals experiencing homelessness. While I always wanted to do something, I would typically react to these people by averting my gaze, pretending to be occupied with my phone, or, upon accidental eye contact, exchanging a timid smile.

On this particular day, my friend Nina joined me on my weekly grocery shopping ritual. As Nina and I approached the bridge over Rock Creek that leads into Foggy Bottom, Nina said out of the blue, "Let's stop and talk to him."

At first, I wasn't sure which "him" she was referring to. The early Sunday morning street was relatively vacant, aside from a few joggers and local residents walking with their strollers and dogs.

And then I understood. He was sitting on a milk crate on the sidewalk at the beginning of the bridge, sporting a hat in the crisp fall breeze and hunching over a folded-out newspaper, with a paper cup by his side.

Realizing the meaning behind Nina's words, my mind flooded with thoughts. *What would I say? What would we possibly have in common to talk about? How would I approach this conversation in a way that wasn't degrading or presumptuous or privileged or worse...?*

As we got closer, I noticed that he was wearing a Green Bay Packers skull cap.

"Can we sit with you?" Nina asked, while I stood hesitantly behind her.

"As long as you don't mind the ground," he responded, notably perplexed by our request.

We sat in silence for what felt like an eternity before Nina started to talk again.

"I'm Nina," she began. "And I'm Clara," I said in turn.

"And I'm Andre," he added, continuing to read his newspaper with an apparently deep level of concentration and an amused grin. I wondered if the grin was in reference to the newspaper's contents or the two girls who had chosen to sit next to him.

Mothers with children and other passersby on the bridge's sidewalk craned their necks at the sight of two white girls wearing Georgetown shirts sitting on the ground with a black homeless man. My face became hot at their gaze.

"What brings you here?" he asked without looking up from his newspaper, unfazed by the observers.

Upon hearing our response, he looked up from his newspaper for the first time. He was amused to hear that we had woken up early on a Sunday morning to walk to a grocery store more than a mile away from our school.

Within a few more minutes the three of us were laughing and talking like old friends, and I forgot my previous inhibitions. What I had built up in my mind to be an uncomfortable encounter with a stranger turned out to be no more than a relaxed conversation with a wise new acquaintance.

The longer we talked to Andre, the more we realized how intimately he knew Washington, D.C. Andre, 52 years old at the time of our conversation, grew up in the Adams Morgan neighborhood of D.C. and spent his childhood days at George-town's Rose Park Playground, one of few integrated parks in the city at the time. He had lived in Washington for his entire life, but after his wife divorced him, he was left with nothing. He told us about his continued search for employment, and his smile lit up as he talked about a job interview he had scheduled for the next day. At the same time, I sensed a hint of discouragement as he acknowledged the difficulties of finding a job in his 50s.

After spending nearly an hour talking to each other, we had to end the conversation in order for Andre to be able to watch the Packers' game. We all reluctantly said good-bye, parting with smiles on our faces.

Nearly every week for the rest of the semester on the way to purchase groceries, I would stop to talk to Andre, both with and without Nina. The more I talked to him, the more I realized that he was one of the most wise and perceptive individuals I had ever met. We discussed everything from the history of the neighborhood and sports to Georgetown's Jesuit values and current events.

I learned firsthand that homelessness is an issue that can affect anyone. As of January 2016, there were more than 8,350 people experiencing homelessness in Washington, D.C. In other words, there were 124 homeless people for every 10,000

Washington, D.C., residents. From 2009 to 2016 alone, the District's homeless population increased by 34 percent, while the national homeless population decreased by 12.9 percent over the same time period. At the same time, Washington's wealth exploded, with real estate prices soaring and the city cementing its status as one of the top 10 cities for millionaires per capita.

These figures illustrate yet another way in which the nation's capital is considered one of the most unequal cities in the United States.

"Homelessness knows no race, gender, or age, affecting nearly every group imaginable. There are certain categories of people, however, who bear this burden at a higher rate," according to an article in *Street Sense*, a publication with the goal of empowering persons experiencing homelessness to succeed through a variety of media platforms.

While black people and African-Americans comprise 25 percent of D.C.'s population, they make up 71 percent of the District's homeless population, a statistic that highlights the systemic factors at play in the District's high homeless population. In Washington, D.C., the disproportionate ratio of the $12.5 hourly minimum wage to the $33.58 wage needed to rent a two-bedroom home further reinforces cycles of poverty and homelessness. There is no quick fix to the complex issue of homelessness, but walking has the power to set collaborative solutions in motion.

"When you're in your car with the window rolled up you don't have to interact with the person experiencing homelessness on the street. But in the situation where you're walking and interacting repeatedly, those barriers begin to break down," says Adam Ducker, informed by his background in real estate.

From personal experience, Adam (who you'll learn more about in Step 8) hypothesizes that volunteer activity is higher in walkable neighborhoods. With real estate experience spanning communities with a wide range of differences in walkability, he believes that there is a higher level of acceptance of resources such as food kitchens and low-income housing in more walkable neighborhoods. When people interact in the more personal context of walking in the same physical space, there is a greater sense of a shared experience.

From Andre, I learned that any long-term solution regarding homelessness requires first acknowledging the systemic forces behind homelessness. With a better understanding of those systemic causes, programs and policies can be more effectively designed to promote solutions such as employment and access to affordable housing.

Washington, D.C., is making strides in confronting its

disproportionately large homeless population. Instrumental in this is the Housing First program, which places individuals experiencing chronic homelessness in permanent housing without preconditions such as sobriety or treatment. For those stuck in a cycle of homelessness, Housing First is a more sustainable solution. Housing First, which costs up to an estimated $23,000 less per person per year than a shelter program, allows people to exit homelessness quickly and has a high retention rate.

Regardless of the progress, there is still a long way to go to confront the systemic causes of homelessness. Walking offers the opportunity to engage directly with individuals experiencing homelessness in order to learn more about their needs. It also provides the chance to build genuine relationships and collaboratively brainstorm solutions to the complex problems of inequality facing society.

Had I not walked past Andre on that one Sunday morning and had Nina not facilitated that conversation, I would have continued down the path of averting my gaze when walking past individuals experiencing homelessness. Walking was the gateway into a personal interaction that helped me better understand the complex story of someone who I had previously just passed by.

Although he may have been experiencing homelessness,

Andre's home is very clearly Washington, D.C. He's called the city home for far longer than I have, and I learned about my home from his experience of watching the Georgetown neighborhood grow and change over the years.

Walking is one of the best ways to engage with all of the people who call a place home, recognizing the unique experiences and insight that each individual brings to a place. In a world defined by dichotomies and polarization, walking — something common to the entire human race — is a force of unity.

WALK TOGETHER

"I wasn't a Democrat or a Republican. I was just a human being walking across the country," Dr. John Francis reflects on his walk across the United States.

For 22 years, Dr. Francis — also known as the Planetwalker — relied on walking (and an occasional sailboat ride) as his only form of transportation. For 17 of those years, he was completely silent.

Dr. Francis initially embarked on his silent walking journey as a form of environmental protest after witnessing an oil spill near the Golden Gate Bridge in San Francisco, which you'll learn more about in Step 7. While he did expect to experience nature and have time for introspection during his walk, an unanticipated aspect of this journey was meeting people from all walks of life on the way.

His commitment to walking and silence was radically countercultural. While this behavior might seem like it would have further isolated Dr. Francis, it actually allowed him to better connect with the people he met on his journey.

Walking and silence both reflect a departure from the fast-paced speed of daily life. Walking provides a literal change of pace, requiring you to reduce your speed from that of an automobile and permitting you to be more present in your surroundings. In a similar way, silence offers the opportunity to shift your conversational role away from the active role of the speaker to the more passive role of the listener.

During the seven years that it took Dr. Francis to trek across America, he walked alongside highways, winding roads, and trails, taking time to notice the idiosyncrasies of the landscape that often go unnoticed by passersby in motorized vehicles, including local flora and fauna. While he was alone for much of the time spent on the road, Dr. Francis was deeply reliant on the aid of others in order to complete his cross-country trip.

Walking through areas as diverse as remote wilderness, large cities, and charming towns, some of Dr. Francis' fondest memories of his walking journey were not of the time he spent alone but instead of the time he spent with the people he met along the way. In the absence of spoken words, he carried around a card with a description about himself and his mission and depended on the hospitality of the complete strangers who welcomed him into their homes. He experienced the incredible generosity of people who invited him to join them for dinner or to spend the night at their house.

During his travels across America, Dr. Francis' view of the country was completely transformed by simple conversations he had with the people he met throughout his journey.

"Flying from one coast to the other and thinking I knew what America was wasn't a very appropriate feeling," he reflects.

Dr. Francis acknowledges that from a bird's eye view, it is easy to see America in terms of red states and blue states, without taking the time to consider the diversity of belief and experience that exists within each state. However, by walking, Dr. Francis was able to encounter each person as an individual with a unique story and perspective.

"All of the people in all of the states were just the people to me," he says. Dr. Francis found that his walking mission was nonpartisan, gaining support from people of all backgrounds and political creeds.

In walking alongside people of diverse backgrounds and silently participating in conversations with them, he discovered that he could gain a deeper understanding of the origins of and reasons behind individuals' beliefs.

"Most of my adult life I have not been listening fully," he reflects in his book *Planetwalker*. "I only listened long enough to determine whether the speaker's ideas matched my own. If they didn't, I would stop listening, and my mind would race ahead to compose an argument against what I believed the speaker's idea or position to be."

He found that silent listening afforded him a new degree of understanding of people whose political opinions conflicted with his own. As he walked across the country, he spread a message of unity, accumulating stories of the diversity of the American experience along the way.

∗ ∗ ∗

One Saturday morning, after learning about and becoming enamored with Dr. Francis' experience, I had the chance to speak with him over the phone. During our conversation, I couldn't help but think of all of the times I hadn't listened fully. Focusing instead on what I would say next, I would only half-listen. Viewing the conversation through the lens of my own experience, I would try to fill in the gaps of what the other person said with my own thoughts, rather than wholeheartedly listening to what the other person had to say.

"What's your favorite place you have visited in all of your years of walking?" I asked Dr. Francis, consciously preparing to listen to his response without distraction.

He paused. *Could I have asked a question that stumped this brilliant man?* I thought.

"I don't have a favorite place. Just right here, right now," he responded with confidence. "If I didn't take that step or go through that town, I wouldn't have been able to go through the next town." Throughout his journey, Dr. Francis gained a personal appreciation for each place he visited, which he shared via photos and presentations with the people he encountered throughout the following steps of his journey.

The longer he traveled, the more his reputation as "the walking man" preceded him. Throughout his journey, Dr. Francis stopped at schools along the way, spreading the impact of his activism among young Americans. In his silent school presentations, he played the banjo, mimed, and shared pictures of his journey, inspiring students and teachers alike with his non-controversial message of environmental preservation and shared humanity. He encouraged students to consider big questions of the mark they were leaving on the world, and his walking journey became symbolic of a larger movement of environmental and social change. At the conclusion of his presentations, he fondly remembers school students, teachers, and staff congregating outside the schools to wish him the best for the continuation of his journey.

Some of the children he encountered through school visits on his journey — now adults — reach out via phone or email, reminding him of just how memorable his walking journey was.

"Did you expect to have such a lasting impact?" I ask.

"I didn't realize the extent of my impact at the time," Dr. Francis reflects. "But it was a big deal. How many Planetwalkers are you going to meet in your life?"

* * *

When teaching in his own classroom in the university setting, Dr. Francis adopted a methodology of silently walking along with his students, being present for their educational journey but not forcing them to think a certain way. In his TED Talk, "Walk the Earth," Dr. Francis describes instances in which he was trying to mime during a class discussion and his class tried to guess what he was attempting to convey.

"Sometimes I would make a sign, and they said things I absolutely did not mean, but I should have. And so what came to me is, if you were a teacher and you were teaching, if you weren't learning you probably weren't teaching very well."

The mindset of a teacher walking alongside his or her students is instructive for the education process. Walking together — rather than one party leading the other — offers an opportunity to enhance learning for both parties. The power of walking and learning together extends beyond the realm of education.

Dr. Francis now works as a public representative as Town Commissioner of West Cape May, New Jersey. In this role, he regularly walks throughout his neighborhood in order to better understand the area and the people he represents. While walking in the community, he has the chance to stop and talk to community members and hear about their needs firsthand. For Dr. Francis, walking provides a way to comprehend the unique experiences of the individuals in his district.

Inspired by his journey and the people he met along the way, Dr. Francis developed Planetwalk, an organization that "fosters connections between young people, scientists, and environmental practitioners." While at the time of his journey Dr. Francis was unique in his status as a Planetwalker, Planetwalk strives to develop a global network of Planetwalkers, building a diverse community centered around walking. Through Planetwalk and the walks it sponsors nationally and internationally, people ranging in age from 11 to 82 have joined in Dr. Francis' mission and discovered the transformative potential of walking together. By promoting environmental responsibility and world peace, Planetwalk continues the powerful work of Dr. Francis' years of walking.

Dr. Francis' experience navigating the world as a Planetwalker demonstrates that if you listen, the way you only can when you're walking alongside someone, you can understand the other person and their experience in an unparalleled way. This kind of experience can change your own world in ways that you never could have imagined.

A PILGRIM'S JOURNEY

"All of my things are packed away in a friend's house.

All I have is a 25-pound backpack to get me by for the next few months.

All I'm doing for the next five weeks is walking."

Jason Nellis' post on Medium the day he began his month-long pilgrimage on the Camino de Santiago reflects his uncertainty about what the next month would hold. By the end of the pilgrimage, he discovered that walking — an activity he believed would become monotonous after five weeks — was a vehicle for better understanding himself and the world around him.

* * *

Jason, a marketer, public speaker, entrepreneur, and member of the team that built Hulu, is accustomed to feeling passionate about and inspired by his work. While working for a content marketing agency in Washington, D.C., however, he began to question if it was time to take his career in a different direction. After deciding to quit his job, Jason faced another difficult decision: what to do next.

Rather than immediately try to search for a new job, he decided to take a step back.

Having grown up in a multi-faith household with a Jewish father and a Catholic mother, religion played an important role in Jason's life. On a family vacation one year prior, Jason and his mom, step-dad, and younger brother had all hiked an abbreviated version of the Camino, and he had been itching to return to complete the full 500-mile pilgrimage from the eastern to the western edge of northern Spain.

"This is probably the last time in my life as an adult where I will have the ability to just go travel with no one telling me otherwise," he thought as he considered dropping everything to go on the pilgrimage.

And so, he decided to embark on the longest pilgrimage route in Europe. First popularized during the Middle Ages, the Camino was designed as a way to reach the city of Santiago, the site of the tomb of the Christian martyr Saint James. While the historical purpose of the Camino was inherently religious, people from around the world now embark on the pilgrimage for a plethora of reasons, primarily spiritual and recreational.

"Everyone has the superficial reason why you go and the deeper reason why you go," Jason says of his experience on the Camino.

As he had declared on social media before starting the pilgrimage, his superficial reason was "to figure out what I want to be when I grow up." By the end of his month-long journey, he had answered a much more important question: "Who do I want to be when I grow up?"

Compared with some of the other ways to make an impact through walking, Jason admits that a month-long hike seems like an inherently individualistic endeavor.

"In a very strange way, the greater good ends up being your

own personal growth," Jason acknowledges. "For the first time in my adult life I could put everything on hold for a minute and just think about the things that were important to me."

Throughout his pilgrimage, Jason contemplated his career, relationships, and personal priorities. He found that the act of walking during the pilgrimage opened his mind and accelerated his thoughts, an experience he likens to "shower thoughts."

"You know when you get in the shower," Jason relates, "and your brain is going and going and the water hits you and you're shampooing and suddenly you have this inspirational moment where you think, 'Oh my gosh, that's how I should have said that!' Your brain is somewhere else and it allows you to relax enough to have the thought that you wanted to have earlier and to connect the things that were otherwise unconnected. To me, the Camino was like a four-week shower."

Professor Ellen Badone, an ethnographer and pilgrimage researcher, agrees that walking in the context of a pilgrimage provides for an unprecedented level of mental clarity. After participating in the Tro Breiz, a walking pilgrimage in Brittany, France, she learned the value of moving at a reduced pace. Walking — as opposed to other modes of transportation — literally makes you adopt a slower speed of life.

"Society moves too fast. We don't take the time to actually get to know people," she believes. "A walking pilgrimage forces you to take time to talk to the people you're with, to appreciate landscapes and things that you otherwise would go by so quickly that you don't even see them."

In one of Professor Badone's research studies, she investigates pilgrimages to the Holy Land and the multiple degrees of meaning these journeys hold for people of different faiths. For Jews, Jerusalem is the capital city of King David's kingdom and the location of the Temple, of which remains today the Western Wall. For Christians, Jesus Christ died, was buried, and rose from the dead in Jerusalem, the birthplace of the Church. For Muslims, Jerusalem is where Muhammad ascended to heaven from the Temple Mount.

It's these varied meanings drawn from the same place, Professor Badone argues, that pave the way for religious conflict.

While the Middle East remains rocked by religiously motivated violence, there's something beautiful about people of different faiths embarking on journeys to the same place and peacefully coexisting — and even growing in faith together. In particular, interfaith pilgrimages to the Holy Land permit pilgrims to walk together and gain a deeper understanding of each other's faith backgrounds. Although these interfaith pilgrimages alone cannot be expected to heal thousands of years of violence and misunderstanding, the practice of walking alongside and engaging in dialogue with people of different faiths provides a model for navigating interfaith relationships in today's world in a peaceful manner.

* * *

For Jason, his walking pilgrimage was a humbling experience of being completely reliant on his own feet and on those around him. Although Jason had originally planned to walk the Camino by himself, he and seven other people he met at the beginning of the pilgrimage ended up staying together throughout the entire journey. From these new friends from around the world, Jason had the opportunity to see the world from another point of view.

"The pilgrimage reminded me that we are not all of my perspective," Jason reflects. "The world is a larger place, and we lose track of how we fit into that larger world."

It was also a reminder of his own limitations. At one point, Jason experienced shin splints so debilitating that he had to stay behind his group for a few days in order to rest his legs before being able to continue his journey. For Jason, being a pilgrim was a humbling experience, best described by the Camino de Santiago's website:

"Numerous emperors like Charlemagne, popes like Callixtus

II, kings like Alfonso II, brave knights like the Spanish "El Cid" or the Knights Templar, noblemen, thousands of priests, farmers, beggars, travelers, the healthy, the sick, the blind, the lame, the rich, and the homeless — all of them were pilgrims in el Camino de Santiago and all of them were treated the same, because no one knew if the dirty, tired, and blistered pilgrim that just arrived in the village before sunset was a king, a bishop, or a pauper."

While walking with his newfound companions, Jason reconsidered his place in the world. Thanks to the greater clarity afforded to him by his pilgrimage and his new friendships, he ultimately decided to apply to jobs on the West Coast. Now, he happily works as the Head of Marketing for Packagd, a family of mobile shopping apps.

Pilgrimages are proof that understanding the world and your place in it often requires being displaced, letting your feet guide you to people and places you never could have imagined.

———

Peace doesn't happen overnight. In a world with more than seven billion people with deeply rooted beliefs and unique personal experiences in 195 countries, the gaps between individuals sometimes seem more like gorges that are impossible to traverse. Walking is a pivotal first step towards the kinds of encounters that turn enemies into allies, adversaries into advocates, and strangers into friends. This slow process of changing hearts and minds offers hope for a more peaceful world.

STEP 5.

POWER TO THE PEDESTRIANS

———

242 miles.

25 days.

484,000 steps.

On March 12, 1930, Mahatma Gandhi departed from a religious retreat in Sabarmati, India, wearing a homemade white shawl and sandals and carrying a walking stick. With the ultimate destination of Dandi, a coastal town on the Arabian Sea, the goal of Gandhi's journey was to oppose the unjust British salt laws. These laws forbade Indians from producing or selling their own salt and imposed a steep tax on salt that disproportionately negatively impacted the country's poorest individuals.

What started as a small group of Gandhi and a few dozen followers escalated to more than 2,500 people by the time the march reached the Arabian Sea. In each village along the 240-mile journey from Sabarmati to Dandi, Gandhi offered powerful speeches in favor of Indian independence to crowds of tens of thousands of people, inspiring impoverished Indians to join the peaceful protest movement. At some points, the march stretched more than two miles long.

Sixty years old at the time of the Salt March, Gandhi was well conditioned to walking. Committed to living a simple life, his lifelong passion for walking began when he was in high school. When he was attending law school in London, he was accustomed to walking eight to 10 miles per day to save money on transportation expenses.

During the Salt March, he consistently walked at a rate of 10 miles per day.

The march, now known as the Salt March or Dandi March, quickly gained national and international attention. Although a long geographic distance from India, Ohio's *Marion Star* published an article entitled, "March for Indian Freedom Launched: 20,000 Witness Start of Gandhi and Disciples in

Campaign Against British Crown," on March 12, 1930. *The New York Times* wrote about the Salt March on an almost daily basis, with the march's conclusion earning two consecutive front-page articles on April 6 and 7, 1930. Around the world, the momentum of Gandhi and his fellow Indians' steps was difficult to ignore.

"My ambition is no less than to convert the British people through non-violence and thus make them see the wrong they have done to India," Gandhi wrote in the days leading up to the march's arrival at the Arabian Sea.

Upon arriving in Dandi, with the eyes of the world watching, Gandhi collected a handful of salt in an act of nonviolent civil disobedience. His action inspired supporters from across India to launch the "Salt Satyagraha," a weeks-long protest in which Indians traveled to the seaside to illegally harvest and sell salt. Throughout the protest, more than 80,000 people, including Gandhi, were arrested for their actions. Despite the nonviolent nature of the movement, many people were beaten by police.

While the salt laws were by no means the only oppressive practice by the British, salt became an important symbol of British oppression and the movement for Indian independence. Contained in its land and water, salt was inherent to India's identity. British control of the resource was a perfect symbol of the repressive control of a foreign power, as it limited Indians' power to use and benefit from a resource that formed an integral part of India's identity.

Although India remained a British colony until 1947, the Salt March was an important step on the road to independence. After Gandhi was released from prison in January 1931, he met with the viceroy of India, Lord Irwin, to negotiate the end of the salt tax and the release of the political prisoners. With the promise of representing the Indian National Congress, a nationalist organization, at a London conference on India's future, Gandhi agreed to call off the Salt Satyagraha. The momentum spurred by the Salt March legitimized the Indian independence movement.

Less than six months after India was granted independence, Gandhi was assassinated by a Hindu extremist at the age of 78. Gandhi's powerful example of walking as a form of protest lives on and has inspired generations of activists, including Martin Luther King, Jr., who led a march from Selma to Montgomery in protest of the South's racist policies.

When people walk together as a unified group, it magnifies the power of their individual steps, turning their steps into a movement and paving the way for lasting change.

Just as Gandhi led a protest against the unjust laws imposed by

British rule, individuals today have the power to join together and walk to protest injustice. In each of the following cases, you'll learn about some of the people who are walking to counter today's complex problems.

MAKING HERSTORY

"Don't get frustrated, get involved. Don't complain, organize."

Maryum Ali's words echo through the Constitution Avenue crowd, where nearly one million women and men of all ages and backgrounds flood the streets for the 2017 Women's March on Washington. Maryum — the eldest daughter of Muhammad Ali, a famously outspoken activist — is a gang prevention activist, and her words have captivated the attention of the impassioned crowd.

"So many people binge-watch television for hours and hours," she continues. "They're in their telephones, they're on their computers on Facebook for hours ... they'll stand up for their sports teams, they know every rule of the NBA and the NFL, but they don't know how local government works. We have to start spending time and being respectful for all humanity and stand up for equal rights."

In the aftermath of the tumultuous 2016 United States election, Maryum's message — and the overarching message of the Women's March — is simple and bipartisan: get informed and do something.

I usually don't like crowds, but being shoulder-to-shoulder with hundreds of thousands of people from all walks of life is awe-inspiring. The throngs of people are gathered to advocate for legislation and policies relating to issues that overwhelmingly impact women, including women's rights, violence prevention, reproductive rights, LGBTQIA rights, immigration reform, workers' rights, environmental justice, healthcare reform, freedom of religion, and racial equality. Political beliefs aside, I feel an intense sense of patriotism as I witness the power of freedom of speech in action. In the face of their rights being threatened, the people gathered for the Women's March react by joining their voices to make a change.

Once the organized program of speeches by celebrities, activists, and government representatives has concluded, there's hardly any room to march down Constitution Avenue, as the Women's March turnout has more than tripled attendance expectations. When at long last it is our turn to march, my friends and I follow the crowd of poster-yielding individuals. Together, we form a unified wave that floods the National Mall and rushes towards our ultimate destination: 1600 Pennsylvania Avenue.

With almost five million participants in nearly 700 marches

on all seven continents as of May 2018, the Women's March gives a physical presence to women's causes. This show of solidarity and determination to affect change is difficult to ignore. As the Women's March Twitter page proudly states, "We're still here. We're not going anywhere."

* * *

More than a year after the first Women's March, I have the chance to learn about the behind-the-scenes of the March from one of the organizers, Breanne Butler. Along with her fellow Women's March organizers, Breanne took on the responsibility of organizing in addition to her day job. She's also a chef in New York City and the CEO of by Breanne, a fashion and food business specializing in candy jewelry. In the male-dominated restaurant industry, Breanne has always been an advocate for women, especially in terms of equal pay and sexism in the workplace.

After hearing the results of the 2016 presidential election, Breanne was so shaken that she had to get off the train from her evening commute to vomit in a trash can. She encountered three other women doing the same thing.

"A lot of women wanted to find some sort of action that they could do so that they could feel better about what was happening," Breanne remarks about the aftermath of the election.

The Women's March did just that. After stumbling upon the Women's March event on Facebook, Breanne messaged the page's organizers, asking, "What can I do?" Although accustomed to organizing kitchens, Breanne soon found herself applying her skills in a new way: organizing marches. As a new member of the Women's March planning committee, she managed the Facebook pages for all of the states that wanted to mobilize to the nation's capital for the march. Within hours of her assuming the role, the March event went viral and Breanne began to receive messages like hers from women around the globe asking how they could contribute.

"What is it that makes walking a particularly impactful form of activism?" I ask Breanne of her experience organizing the Women's March.

"There's power in movement," she responds immediately.

"Literally, these things are called movements," she adds. "When you're actually putting out energy with so many other like-minded people by exercising and literally shaking the atoms between each person, it's pretty powerful."

While the 2017 marches in Los Angeles, Chicago, and New York City drew in crowds numbering in the hundreds of thousands, one march in the 65-person Nova Scotia village of Sandy Cove had only 15 attendees: 12 women, two men, and one toddler. Still, nearly 200,000 people have viewed a short video of the participants enthusiastically waving their signs along a Nova Scotian highway on the two-mile march route. Regardless of size, each gathering of like-minded people has an impact, with the Women's March sending a message that women are a force to be reckoned with.

Following in the example of Mahatma Gandhi's nonviolent protest, not one arrest was made in the course of all of the Women's Marches. The Women's March organizers credit social media with setting the standard for this peaceful protest — and for helping organize an entire movement in just 10 weeks.

"There's no way we would have been able to pull off something like Women's March without technology," Breanne says. "Still, social media is great for a quick fix, but long-term building is a face-to-face thing."

In order to change policy and promote lasting change, according to Breanne, the in-person element of a physical march is essential. While it's relatively easy to reply "Going" to an event on Facebook, it takes a much more concerted effort to attend a physical march. Being physically present and walking with other people in a space opens up new possibilities for collaboration and understanding among participants of varied backgrounds.

"Doing things like marches makes you realize how much you do have in common, how much more unites us than divides us," Breanne says.

In keeping with this message of unity, inclusivity is at the core of the Women's March. While it bears the name "Women's March," the march is for all people whose rights might be threatened, including immigrants, religious groups, people with disabilities, and those who identify as LBGTQIA.

"One of the biggest takeaways from Women's March is that women of color have been organizing for a very long time because they had to in their communities," Breanne reflects. "What was so cool about Women's March was that we had women of color leading this and really making key decisions, and being a face of the march, and that really welcomed other communities to come in."

From the perspective of economic accessibility, the Women's March prioritized helping local groups fundraise so that the high price of airfare to D.C. for the weekend of the March was not a barrier to entry for women of diverse socioeconomic statuses.

"We're focused on inclusion, intersectionality, standing with people with disabilities, standing with the most marginalized," Breanne asserted in an interview with the digital magazine *Dazed*.

The Women's March provides an example of large-scale organizing in a short window of time, with particular focuses on inclusivity and channeling the power of technology. While the work of the Women's March is far from finished, the Women's March has effectively provided a unified outlet for previously disparate voices, amplifying the impact of individuals' actions.

As we near the end of our conversation, Breanne reflects, "Coming from the food industry where you work really hard and see instant results in the form of a good meal or a happy customer and then to be in a space where you know you're doing life-changing, world-changing work but you're chipping away at it very slowly, it's important to keep your eye on the prize and make sure you know that you're contributing and doing something important and also not to burn out. There's going to be mistakes made and hard things are going to come, but you'll get through it knowing that your work is literally changing someone's life."

TAKE A WALK. JOIN A MOVEMENT.

"Why are black women dying faster and at higher rates than any other group of people in America from preventable obesity-related diseases?" GirlTrek co-founders Vanessa Garrison and T. Morgan Dixon ask in their inspirational and action-oriented TED Talk, "The Trauma of Systematic Racism is Killing Black Women. A First Step Toward Change…"

Vanessa's grandmother died from a heart attack at the young age of 66, when Vanessa was 13. Throughout her life, Vanessa's grandmother tirelessly cared for 11 children, many more grandchildren, and her entire community. However, she sacrificed her own health in the process, struggling with her weight and with chronic illnesses. Vanessa began to notice a pattern in her family when her two of her aunts passed away at the ages of 55 and 63 from what could have been preventable causes. Calculating the average life expectancy of women in her family, Vanessa was astonished to discover that her female relatives lived to be only 65. The average life expectancy in the United States is 79.

Meanwhile, 53 percent of black women are also obese, and 82 percent are over a healthy weight. Half of black girls will get diabetes if they do not change their diets. Every day in America, 137 black women die from heart disease, a preventable illness.

"And no one is talking about it," Vanessa says matter-of-factly.

Determined to change these statistics, Vanessa and her friend Morgan founded GirlTrek, now the largest public health nonprofit for African-American women and girls in the United States. With GirlTrek, women sign a pledge to walk for just 30 minutes per day, five days per week. Through neighborhood walking programs, GirlTrek inspires women to take a first step towards healthier lives, families, and communities.

While these health statistics are an apparent surface issue for black women, Vanessa and Morgan realize that there are deeper problems at play. Health and weight problems are a symptom of generations of systemic racism, from divestment in schools and predatory housing prices to mass incarceration and a cocaine epidemic. Obesity and inactivity stem from deeper concerns about community safety and historical trauma. As a result, GirlTrek goes beyond a fitness-only approach to provide black women with a strong community support system as well as training for organizing and problem-solving.

"For black women whose bodies are buckling under the weight of systems never designed to support them, GirlTrek is a lifeline," Vanessa promises.

Vanessa believes that the solution to the problems faced by black women must be grounded in women's own communities. Following the example of generations of black women, Girl-Trek embraces walking as the way to empower women and create lasting change, and it makes use of grapevine techniques of information-sharing that have been at play in the successful movements of the past. On the Underground Railroad, Harriet Tubman and other conductors walked slaves to freedom through a network of secret routes and safe houses. In the

1950s Montgomery Bus Boycott, walking was the alternate form of transportation through which African-Americans in Montgomery, Alabama, were able to fulfill the pledge, "We will not ride."

"From Harriet Tubman to the women in Montgomery, when black women walk, things change," Morgan declares.

GirlTrek asserts that walking is the single most powerful thing a woman can do for her body. But the positive impact of walking isn't only physical.

"Once walking, those women get to organizing — first their families and then their communities — to walk and solve problems together," Vanessa observes in the TED Talk. "They walk and notice the abandoned building, they walk and notice the lack of sidewalks, the lack of green space... and they say, 'No More.'"

Susie Page, a Philadelphia resident and member of GirlTrek's Team Nazarene, is an example of Vanessa's words in action. During Team Nazarene's walks in their North Philadelphia neighborhood, Susie and the team noticed that an abandoned building and parking lot near their local church was covered with graffiti and had become a dumping ground for old furniture, appliances, and trash.

"We kept calling the city, but they never did anything," Susie remarked in an interview with online publication *Philly Powered*.

Led by Susie, Team Nazarene decided to take charge and organize a cleanup of the neighborhood eyesore. Susie and the team continue to walk the neighborhood year-round, monitoring the abandoned lot that they cleaned and looking out for other neighborhood spots in need of attention.

"I can't help but wonder what would happen if there were groups of women walking on Trayvon's block [the day he died], or what would happen in the South Side of Chicago every day if there were groups of women and mothers and aunts and cousins walking, or along the polluted rivers of Flint, Michigan," Morgan says in the TED talk, imagining the potential impact of walking. "I believe that walking can transform our communities, because it's already starting to."

In order to enact the kind of change envisioned by GirlTrek, Vanessa and Morgan welcome all people to join GirlTrek's mission of promoting individual and community health. Walking is affordable and accessible, and it's a great place to start for anyone regardless of their baseline fitness level.

The Project for Public Spaces concurs: "Walking is for everyone — no matter if you live in an inner city neighborhood or a suburb without sidewalks or a rural community, no matter whether you are out of shape or a youngster or roll in a wheelchair."

The founders encourage integrating walking into daily life, from running errands to taking a break from work, but they recognize that walkability is a luxury for many. As a result, they advocate for deliberate urban planning that makes walking a safer and more convenient option for more people.

As of 2018, GirlTrek has more than 100,000 neighborhood walkers, with the goal of getting one million people in the 50 most vulnerable communities in the United States to sign the pledge to move. In often-matriarchal African-American families, mobilizing women to get moving also mobilizes their families. All of these people walking together has the power to uplift entire communities.

"We're walking so we can be healthy enough to stand on the front lines for change in our communities," Vanessa and Morgan assert in the talk.

The GirlTrek guidebook, aptly named *Harriet's Handbook*, makes clear the interconnectedness of walking, self-care, and changing the world, quoting American writer Audre Lorde: "Caring for myself is not self-indulgence; it is self-preservation. And that is an act of political warfare."

HOW MOVEMENTS HAPPEN

Movements don't happen overnight.

As shown by Gandhi's many public appearances along his journey, the extensive preparation of the Women's March planners, and the grapevine mobilization by the GirlTrek founders, building a movement requires strategic planning and collaboration. Walking is just one — albeit important — component of building a greater movement capable of creating lasting change.

The March for Our Lives is an ideal illustration of how movements happen. Held on March 24, 2018 in the aftermath of the Stoneman Douglas High School shooting in Parkland, Florida, the March for Our Lives was spearheaded by classmates of the shooting's victims. The march had clear demands: universal background checks on all gun sales, raising the federal age of gun ownership and possession to 21, and restoring the 1994 Federal Assault Weapons Ban.

In the days leading up to the March for Our Lives, as Washington, D.C., prepared for an influx of protestors against gun violence, I attended a Georgetown University panel entitled, "How Movements Happen," that analyzed the characteristics that make movements successful. The panel featured five experienced change-makers: Colleen Roberts, a recent Georgetown graduate and Black Lives Matter activist; Leslie

Crutchfield, the executive director of Georgetown's Global Social Enterprise Initiative; David Cole, the national legal director for the American Civil Liberties Union; Sarah Clements, a Georgetown senior and gun reform activist; and Leticia Bode, a Georgetown professor of communication, culture and technology.

Leslie Crutchfield, the author of *How Change Happens: Why Some Movements Succeed While Others Don't*, was the first person on the panel to speak.

"The most important factor that differentiates winning movements from the rest are the grassroots — how they mobilize and organize and work city by city, state by state to move the country closer to their ideal," she asserted, echoing the best practices of the three movements already discussed. The National Rifle Association (NRA), Leslie said, is particularly effective at grassroots organizing. Prior to pushing for national legislation, it first focuses on cultivating strong local chapters with active members.

According to Leslie, movements are most successful when they build on each other. In this way, the March for Our Lives has benefitted from following in the footsteps of the groundwork laid by gun control organizations Sandy Hook Promise and Everytown for Gun Safety. Leslie believes that the spark of the #NeverAgain movement will catch thanks to the tinder laid out by the movements that preceded it.

Sarah Clements has played a critical role in laying the groundwork for the gun control movement. In 2012, Sarah's mom survived the shooting at Sandy Hook Elementary School in Newtown, Connecticut. Twenty first-graders and six of Mrs. Clements' colleagues were killed. A high school junior at the time of the shooting, Sarah made the conscious decision to dedicate her life to preventing the same kind of suffering that her community had experienced at the hands of gun violence.

"People always say, 'Nothing changed after Sandy Hook,'" Sarah said in an interview with *The Atlantic* released on the day of the March for Our Lives. "And that angers me, because I actually don't think this moment would be happening without the change that happened after Sandy Hook. I think that there was a big culture shift, and a political shift — maybe not necessarily nationally, in terms of policy. I think after Sandy Hook, we forced the country to have a continued national dialogue. We built new organizations. That infrastructure of grassroots organizers in every state and in every community, and funding on these issues, and creating a leadership pipeline for young organizers — those things absolutely did not exist before Sandy Hook."

One of the major takeaways from Sarah's experience in activism is to learn from the communities that have been organizing the longest. Newtown, a white upper-middle-class suburb, quickly gained national attention in the aftermath of the shooting. However, communities of color and of lower socioeconomic status have disproportionately been the victims of gun violence and have been organizing on their own for years without the same degree of media attention.

"We will not win if we don't listen to the communities that have been organizing the longest," Sarah said on the panel, emphasizing the need to build with these communities in an inclusive movement.

When employed strategically, technology can be a tool that amplifies the impact of physical marches. According to Professor Bode, change requires 1) motivation, 2) mobilization, and 3) capacity in the forms of funding and knowledge. As the Women's March organizers learned, social media can impact all of these areas by helping to raise awareness for a cause, facilitating the organization of large groups of people, and providing a platform for fundraising and education. Before, during, and after a march, technology plays a role in coordinating, raising awareness, and sustaining momentum.

While the goal of marches — and movements as a whole — is largely to influence policy, marches can also move the needle in the private sector. In the aftermath of the Parkland school shooting, the survivors publicly called out corporations that invested in the gun lobby. Following the NRA's opposition to banning certain assault weapons and its recommendation to arm teachers to respond to future school shootings, the survivors called for a boycott of the NRA. In the face of public pressure, many companies — including Best Western, Enterprise, and United Airlines — severed ties with the NRA almost immediately.

Changing policy is a lengthier process. Although the March for Our Lives did have clear policy demands, these demands will not be met without continued action. The organizers have developed explicit action steps in order to ensure that the success of the march results in future policy change. The March for Our Lives website channels the buzz surrounding the March into action, with instructions to "Take the next step" by starting a club and most importantly to "Register. Educate. Vote."

While March 24, 2018 was only the beginning of the work of the March for Our Lives, it demonstrated the power of a march in strengthening and unifying a movement. The March for Our Lives proves that when people come together under a unified cause, it has the power to effect chain reactions of change.

"The notion is that you are not born with the DNA for hope, nor are you born with the DNA for apathy or fatalism," said David Cole at the conclusion of the panel. "It is not that hope causes people to act. It is the other way around. If we act, we create hope, and it's also true that if we sit back and spectate, we create fatalism."

———

Beginning with the nonviolent example set by Mahatma Gandhi, these movements demonstrate the power of pedestrians in igniting social change. While individual pedestrians do have an impact when they walk alone, the act of people walking together as a unified group magnifies the impact of each individual's steps. So, if there's something about your world that you think needs to be changed, don't hesitate to take the first step. You never know how many people might follow.

STEP 6.

WALKING FOR A CAUSE

———

As much as I'd like for it to be the case, walking on its own is not enough to tackle some of the world's biggest problems. The challenges we face are varied and complex:

- Cancer is one of the leading causes of death around the world. In 2012, 14.1 million new cases and 8.2 million cancer-related deaths were reported worldwide. By 2030, that number is anticipated to reach 23.6 million.
- Every 98 seconds, an American is sexually assaulted. This means that there are more than 321,000 victims of sexual assault each year in the United States, on average, with the majority of victims under the age of 30.
- More than 750 million people around the world lack access

to clean drinking water. Approximately 2,300 people per day — or 842,000 people per year — die as a result of inadequate drinking water and sanitation.

Unlike the cases of physical and mental health, walking does not have the potential for immediate impact in these issue areas. These problems — like many of the other challenges currently facing the world — are so large and complex that they require the collective and coordinated efforts of many individuals walking together.

While walking alone cannot cure cancer, end sexual assault, or improve access to drinking water, walking is indeed a tool for fundraising in these issue areas. Walking is an incredibly effective and impactful form of fundraising, with current fundraising efforts touching on nearly every problem facing the world. Rooted in a phenomenon you'll soon come to know as the power of reciprocity, walking offers an innovative approach to fundraising by bringing people together, building awareness, and raising the funds required to channel steps into real change.

FUNDRAISING 101

"Pay to the order of: Clara Cecil"

"Amount: One-hundred and no / hundreds dollars. 100 and

0/100"

"For: St. Jude's Math-A-Thon"

* * *

In kindergarten, I made the biggest sale of my young fundraising career. Up until that point, I had never had more than $5 in my possession at any particular moment. And now I had a $100 check with my name on it.

I was scared to hold it, for fear of ripping it or losing it or smudging the perfect cursive ink writing. But I was also proud to know the potential life-changing power of that thin paper rectangle.

Just a few days earlier, my kindergarten teacher, Mrs. Lewis, had introduced our fundraising assignment to the class.

"Through the St. Jude Math-A-Thon, you'll have the chance to raise money for St. Jude's Children's Research Hospital in Memphis, Tennessee," Mrs. Lewis had said. "St. Jude's is a pediatric treatment and research center that focuses on helping kids with catastrophic diseases that require long periods of hospitalization or recovery such as leukemia. As a not-for-profit hospital, St. Jude's never charges families for a child's care."

All I could think about was my pre-school friend's younger sister, Cameron, who was fighting a battle with leukemia. I didn't know a lot about the disease, but I knew that it was bad and that I wanted to raise money to make sure no one else had to deal with the pain Cameron had experienced.

"To raise money, all you have to do is fill out this booklet of math problems in the next month and ask your friends and family to donate to your fundraiser," Mrs. Lewis continued, waving a colorful pamphlet in the air and handing one to each of the 24 students in our class. "And for the highest fundraisers, you'll have the chance to win prizes like this boombox CD player," she added, pointing to a picture of a shiny gray boombox in the prize catalogue.

Thumbing through the book of math problems, I couldn't wait to get started as soon as school got out. *Not only was I going to get to raise money for a good cause,* I thought, *but I was going to get to do extra problems for my favorite subject AND have the chance to win my very own boombox.*

As soon as I got home that afternoon, I ran from our garage to the kitchen and sat down at our wooden table, calculator in hand, to start solving the word problems. Each page presented a puzzle that I couldn't wait to solve. While the math problem booklet was intended to last throughout the month-long campaign, I solved the entire booklet within 48 hours of receiving it.

Immediately after finishing the math problems, I started calling my family and friends to ask for donations. Uncle Michael was the first name on my list.

"Would you like to donate to my St. Jude's Math-A-Thon fundraiser?" I asked politely when he answered the phone.

"How about $100?" he replied immediately.

One hundred dollars? I thought. My piggy bank had accumulated only about $15 in my entire five years of existence.

"Wow! Thank you," I said in disbelief, my mouth forming a huge grin as I tried to imagine such a large sum of money.

One by one, I called my other aunts and uncles and family friends, moving through the lines of my parents' list of approved people to contact and excitedly informing each one of the completion of my Math-A-Thon booklet. Nearly everyone I called was excited to contribute at least a few dollars to the cause of my fundraising campaign. There must have been something about a five-year-old being so excited to do math and to help other kids that elicited the generosity of those I innocently solicited for donations.

At the end of the campaign, all of the parties involved won: I ecstatically received a boombox CD player, my family and friends gained the personal satisfaction of donating to a worthy cause, and St. Jude's used the money in its efforts to provide care free of charge to children such as Cameron undergoing treatment for catastrophic diseases.

Through my small-scale fundraising experience, I learned my first lesson on the power of reciprocity, a practice that still holds true in large-scale fundraising efforts to solve the world's greatest challenges.

WALK FOR LIFE

"I have cancer."

They're the three words that no child ever wants to hear a parent say.

When Greer Richey was a senior in high school, her dad received this devastating diagnosis. In the face of this news, Greer felt powerless. While she was able to provide her dad with emotional support and drive him to medical appointments after he couldn't drive himself, she longed to be able to provide him with the physical care he so desperately needed.

How am I expected to go through the motions of daily life when my dad is fighting for his life? she thought.

Greer resolved to channel her feelings of powerlessness into action. She tried to join her high school's chapter of Relay for Life, the primary fundraising arm for the American Cancer Society. However, the news of her dad's diagnosis came in the spring, after her school had already held its annual Relay for Life event.

About six months after the diagnosis, Greer started college at Georgetown University, where her dad had graduated from medical school 30 years prior. When looking for student organizations to join, Greer discovered Georgetown's chapter of Relay for Life. With walking as a primary component of the organization's fundraising and community-building, Relay seemed like the perfect way to take action.

"It felt like a tangible way to get involved and do something positive for my dad and the cancer community," Greer says. "I wanted to ensure that other people didn't have their lives turned upside down by cancer."

After starting off as a general committee member in 2014, Greer became increasingly involved with Relay for Life throughout each of her four years at Georgetown. During her sophomore year, she coordinated a large portion of Georgetown's Relay event, organizing everything from the event theme and props to games and student performances. As a junior, she was the Mission Co-Chair, which involved coordinating Hope Lodge visits to provide meals for cancer patients and caregivers, as well as planning a celebration dinner for cancer survivors during the Relay event. By her senior year, she served as the President of Georgetown's chapter of Relay for Life, pouring an extensive portion of her time outside of school and work into the organization's year-round fundraising efforts.

Relay for Life's founder, Dr. Gordon Klatt, recognized the unique opportunity for walking to contribute to the fight against cancer. As a colorectal surgeon specializing in cancer, he wanted to find an effective way to support the American Cancer Society's research, education, advocacy, and service. In 1985, Dr. Klatt walked and ran 83.6 miles around a track at the University of Puget Sound in Tacoma, Washington, raising more than $28,000 through pledges from friends, family, and patients during a 24-hour period. The first Relay for Life was held the following year in 1986, raising more than $33,000.

Dr. Klatt lost his own battle with stomach cancer in 2014 at the age of 71, but the fundraising campaign that began with a single man has grown to include more than 5,000 events in 20 countries around the world. As of 2018, Relay for Life has raised more than $5 billion to support the American Cancer Society's mission to "lead the fight for a world without cancer."

Following in the footsteps of Dr. Klatt's initial fundraising campaign, each Relay for Life event ranges in length from six to 24 hours. Walking remains a critical component, with team members taking turns walking around a track for the entirety of the event. While pledging money for laps walked is no longer the organization's only fundraising vehicle, it still plays a central role in each Relay for Life event. Just as doing math problems was a critical component of my Math-A-Thon fundraising success, walking is an integral part of Relay for Life's fundraising efforts, as Greer has learned from her personal fundraising experience.

"Seeing people walking around the track for hours upon hours all night has a big visual impact as well as a physical, mental, emotional, and financial impact," Greer says, acknowledging Relay for Life's unique power as a fundraiser.

In his TED Talk "Are you a giver or a taker?" Adam Grant labels this effect as the "power of reciprocity." He observes that there are three kinds of people in the world: givers, takers, and matchers. While *givers* give freely without expecting anything in return, *takers* act out of self-interest to maximize their personal gains and *matchers* give only when it is the norm or when they recognize an opportunity to gain something in return. He observed that givers fared poorly in many situations — especially in the workplace — because of their willingness to blindly give without being rewarded for their efforts.

Reciprocity, Grant recognized, is the key to achieving better outcomes for all people involved.

"Between 75 and 90 percent of all giving in organizations starts with a request," Grant observes. While some givers — or, in this case, fundraisers who give their time to an organization's mission — are hesitant to engage in unsolicited requests for money, being able to guarantee reciprocity attracts both matchers and other givers to contribute to the fundraiser's mission.

Greer has found that family, friends, and strangers are more willing to donate to Relay when there is a level of reciprocity involved. Donors typically pledge to give a certain amount of money for each lap that a participant walks, with the understanding that the participant must exert more energy in order to walk more laps and earn more funds. The promise of walking to earn donations — as opposed to simply unsolicited fundraising — assures donors that the participant has a greater sense of personal investment that extends beyond the act of fundraising.

For participants, the act of tracking laps walked — whether it is through a tally or through a physical marker such as a bracelet — further reinforces the intentionality of the fundraising and keeps awareness of the cause at the forefront of the fundraiser's mind.

* * *

Along with its fundraising function, Relay for Life plays an essential role in raising awareness and building community. Relay for Life draws a symbolic link between event participants' act of walking and the battle against cancer.

"Cancer patients don't stop because they're tired, and for one night, neither do we," states the Relay for Life website.

A hallmark of the Relay for Life event is the Survivor Lap, in which survivors and people currently affected by cancer walk around the track amidst the cheers of all of the event attendees. Each year, Greer is moved by emotion during the Survivor Lap as she proudly watches her dad, now cancer-free, walking around the track. As the Survivors complete their lap, Caregivers join in with Survivors for a second lap, symbolizing their presence alongside their loved ones during and beyond the journey of fighting cancer.

"I wasn't a caregiver for my dad in the sense that I physically took care of him," Greer says. Still, she joins in the Caregiver Lap each year because of the many other kinds of support she provided for her dad throughout his treatment.

Later in the event, Luminarias, paper bags filled with lights, are dedicated to individuals who have lost the battle to cancer, are currently battling cancer, or have overcome cancer. After the Luminarias are lit, all event attendees join in a silent lap around the track.

"Darkness is symbolic of the fear that a patient feels when diagnosed," according to the American Cancer Society. "After sunset, we light Luminarias to remember those we have lost, to celebrate cancer survivors, and to show those affected by cancer that they are not alone."

The act of walking around the track together, a sign of mutual support, is accessible to people regardless of their ability. Each year people of all abilities join in the lap using wheelchairs, crutches, or canes, or supported by the arms of loved ones.

"There is a way for everyone to participate in Relay for Life, even if they can't physically walk themselves. No matter what you are going through in your personal life you can come together and fight cancer in a unified way," Greer reflects.

Relay for Life has become the defining aspect of Greer's Georgetown experience. Through her fundraising, Greer has had the opportunity to walk alongside her dad and countless other cancer patients and survivors, and her experience with Relay for Life has provided her with a sense of purpose in the face of a feeling of powerlessness. Greer and her dad regularly walk together on the C&O Canal near their home in Arlington,

Virginia, and she remains hopeful that one day we will live in a world where cancer does not exist.

Along with events such as Relay for Life, walking fundraisers such as the Avon Walk for Breast Cancer are a promising tool for raising awareness as well as money, both of which can help make Greer's vision of a world without cancer a reality.

FIGHTING CANCER IS A MARATHON, NOT A SPRINT

"When I grow up, I'm going to be a veterinarian," my cousin Emilie confidently announced when we were kids.

Growing up, she split her free time between riding horses and helping others, whether that meant volunteering at nursing homes and soup kitchens or raising funds for tsunami victims. To me, a career as a veterinarian seemed like the perfect fit between my older cousin's two strongest passions.

When she was eight years old, Emilie's mom was unexpectedly diagnosed with breast cancer. I was barely two years old at the time, so I don't remember the impact of my aunt's illness on our family. I can only imagine how hard it must have been for Emilie and her younger sister Theresa to face the uncertainty of their mom's illness.

As always, Emilie channeled her energy into action. She

continued volunteering in the community in a variety of ways throughout her mom's illness and after her mom won her battle against cancer. Still, Emilie longed to do something more to help cancer victims.

In high school, Emilie learned about the Avon Walk for Breast Cancer, a two-day walk of either 26.2 miles (a marathon) or 39.3 miles (a marathon and a half) that raises funds for breast cancer research, awareness, and education. The money raised also aids the families of people diagnosed with breast cancer.

"The personal aspect of how this disease had affected someone so close to me, coupled with my own hunger to help those in need, propelled me to seek this specific cause out," Emilie reflects.

Each year, the walk — now called "AVON 39 The Walk to End Breast Cancer" — takes place in seven cities across the United States: Boston, Chicago, Houston, New York City, San Francisco, Santa Barbara, and Washington, D.C.

"A large piece of the money stays in the city you walk, so you make a difference in your own community," says Jill Surdyka, a 10-year walk veteran and an AVON 39 National Ambassador.

While the exact percentage of funds raised from each event that is donated to local communities is unclear from Avon's financial reporting, the Avon Foundation's grants are particularly geared towards local-level breast cancer screening and care programs. Since beginning in 2003, the Avon Walks have raised nearly $620 million for local, regional, and national breast cancer organizations.

In order to even qualify to participate in the walk, Emilie had to raise a minimum of $1,800. In addition to preparing through intense fundraising, Emilie had to train to walk a marathon — not an easy feat. Even though Emilie was a high school athlete and had years of volunteering and fundraising experience, both aspects of preparation presented a mental, physical, and financial challenge.

To Emilie, walking is a particularly effective way to raise money and awareness because of its multifaceted approach. Prior to the event, she asked nearly everyone she knew to donate to her fundraiser, spreading awareness along the way. After hearing about her intense preparation to walk the marathon, the people she solicited were more inclined to donate to Emilie's cause — again, a testament to the power of reciprocity in fundraising. Even for those friends, family, or acquaintances who did not donate to her campaign, they still learned more about the cause Emilie was promoting and offered support as she prepared for her walk.

* * *

At long last, the day of the walk arrived. Thousands of women and men came together in Washington, D.C., to march and raise awareness. D.C.'s overwhelmingly gray streets were flooded with people dressed from head-to-toe in pink, carrying pink signs and banners, following behind pink Avon cars, and walking through pink blow-up arches. The explosion of color and passion for the cause was difficult to ignore.

As a high school student at the time, Emilie participated with one of her friends rather than marching alone. While her friend had never been directly affected by anyone who had breast cancer, Emilie found that the experience was equally or more impactful for her friend.

"That one person is now more aware and can spread this awareness to others in the future," Emilie recognizes, thinking of all of the individuals in the crowd who, like her friend, had never been directly impacted by breast cancer.

The walk itself was exhausting. During the two-day event, participants experienced rain, heat, and aching joints. By the time they reached their tents at the end of Day 1, they were physically and mentally worn out.

Emilie went through the two days with a smile. After all, these were the difficulties she had anticipated and agreed upon when she first began her fundraising campaign. As with a battle against cancer, there's no way to fully prepare for all of the unpredictable and uncontrollable challenges presented by the two-day walk. When the going got tough, she found constant inspiration in the joy and enthusiasm of her fellow walk participants.

After completing the marathon walk and surpassing her fundraising goal in 2007, Emilie decided to participate in the Walk for Breast Cancer a second time in 2008. This time, Academy Award-winning actress Reese Witherspoon, the honorary chairwoman of the Avon Foundation, was one of the guest speakers who inspired the 3,500 participants.

"More than anything else, I have faith — faith we will find a cure," Witherspoon said, reflecting on the impact of the walk. "I saw this commitment in the faces of the women in Washington — in the faces of the women walking and the women and men who stood on the sidelines encouraging the 3,500 participants to the finish line. I was cheering right along with them, screaming for action to find a cure."

Together, the acts of walking and fundraising have the power not just to raise awareness but also to put money behind a cause in order to promote lasting change. Events such as the Avon Walk for Breast Cancer provide hope for a future without cancer.

Emilie now works as a critical care nurse at Johns Hopkins Hospital, channeling her passion for helping others in a different way than through her childhood dream of being a veterinarian. Nearly 10 years after participating in the Avon Walk for Breast Cancer, Emilie stills feels that it is an experience that she will never forget.

"When I reminisce about it, it still gives me chills. There were so many beautiful women and men, with so many happy — and not just happy, but joyful! — faces and attitudes. These experiences are the moments that humanity needs. And even if the money doesn't solve anything in the near future, I think that this type of joy and hope is a strong and unique gift to each of us on its own. Maybe even more powerful."

As Emilie discovered, the integrated nature of fundraising, awareness-raising, and community-building makes walking for a cause a particularly transformative method of changing the world. A symbolic connection between the cause and the act of walking only enhances the potential for impact.

WALK A MILE IN THEIR SHOES

"You can't really understand another person's experience until you've walked a mile in their shoes," the saying goes.

Walk a Mile in Her Shoes: The International Men's March to

Stop Rape, Sexual Assault, and Gender Violence allows men to literally walk a mile in women's high-heeled shoes.

"Move your hips and swing your arms for balance," reads the event's instructions for walking in high heels. "Swing your arms. Do not flap them. You cannot fly, though with shoes like these you'll feel like you can soar."

While the event's execution is indeed humorous — just picture throngs of men trying to navigate the streets in red high-heeled shoes — the event participants take the event and the causes it supports very seriously. Walk a Mile in Her Shoes was started by Frank Baird in 2001 after a small group of men decided to raise awareness about men's violence against women by walking around a local park in high-heeled shoes. Now, tens of thousands of people have raised millions of dollars for rape crisis and domestic violence centers, sexualized violence education, and prevention and remediation programs by participating in Walk a Mile in Her Shoes events around the world.

The lighthearted nature of the event provides an entry point into deeper conversations about gender relations and men's sexualized violence against women. The walk facilitates preventative education in order to educate men on issues of rape, sexual assault, and gender violence. Furthermore, the event helps match community members who have experienced domestic violence or sexual assault with resources for recovery.

"A lot of people think domestic violence and sexual assault is a female problem, but it's completely not — it's a human issue," said one male participant at a Walk a Mile in Her Shoes event in Chambersburg, PA.

Through this event, walking provides an avenue for understanding, awareness-raising, and fundraising for treatment and prevention.

* * *

The Project Concern International (PCI) Walk for Water offers another angle on the idea of walking in another person's shoes. Through a 5K walking fundraiser on World Water Day each spring, Walk for Water raises money for clean water solutions, educates the public, and encourages conservation.

While many 5K run/walk events lack a connection between the cause itself and the actual act of running or walking, this is not the case with Walk for Water. Walk participants have the opportunity to carry actual buckets of water, simulating the journey that many people around the world take daily to get clean drinking water. This connection between the cause and the act of walking offers a unique way to understand the cause you are raising money for.

"The reason I love Walk for Water is because we get a feel for what families have to go through every day around the world to support each other and provide for each other," says Sophia Visotcky, one of the high school students on the committee for organizing the 2015 Walk for Water.

Women in developing countries spend up to 10 years of their lives collecting water. The water they transport can weigh up to 44 pounds, significantly heavier than the Home Depot buckets carried on the 5K course. Time spent searching for water — up to six hours per day — means missing out on school or other work, also known as "time poverty." While the Walk for Water course covers more than three miles, people around the world often have to travel double the length of a 5K on much more treacherous terrain in order to have access to clean water.

Walk for Water will never perfectly simulate the actual conditions of transporting water in many developing countries. Still, it helps bridge the gap between places where people make multiple, strenuous trips per day to provide for basic water needs and places that can afford to waste 2.5 gallons of water per minute in the shower. Bringing together the goals of conservation, education, and fundraising has the potential to generate large-scale impact beyond the money raised at the event itself.

"When you ask public health experts what the one thing is that makes the biggest difference in saving lives and giving children a healthier start at life, it's clean water," says NBC7's Mark Mullen, who was the Master of Ceremonies at PCI's 10th Annual Walk for Water at Mission Bay, San Diego. Walk for Water events raise awareness for water solutions as essential components for sustainably fighting global poverty.

The money raised during the Walk for Water event goes directly to improving clean water access for communities. In 2016, for example, PCI partnered with Engineers without Borders to tackle Ethiopia's water crisis. In order to more effectively spend the money, the needs were communicated by the community itself: repairing the community's diesel electric pump and smaller hand pumps. By taking into account the community's self-identified needs, Engineers without Borders was able to extract the highest possible impact out of every dollar raised.

Walk for Water events show that walking isn't just a mechanism for fundraising: It's also a vehicle for understanding the complex issue of global water security. This unique combination of understanding and funding allows resources to be more effectively spent.

———

The power of reciprocity is the driving force that makes walking fundraisers particularly effective. When there's a genuine connection between the act of walking during the fundraising event and the fundraising organization's mission, the potential for impact increases substantially. From Relay for Life to Walk for Water, walking fundraisers prove that walking has the power to build community, raise awareness, and raise money. By putting money behind the causes that people care about, walking fundraisers channel steps into real change in combating global crises as diverse as cancer, sexual assault, and poverty.

PHASE III

A SOCIETAL SHIFT

STEP 7.

THE FOOTPRINT WE LEAVE

———

Global temperatures are swelling. Glaciers are melting. Sea levels are rising. Cities are flooding.

We're in "uncharted territory," warns a March 2017 World Meteorological Organization report.

While all of the earth's inhabitants are already experiencing the effects of climate change, not everyone will be impacted equally. Although the world's wealthiest countries are the highest emitters of greenhouse gases, the world's poorest countries are the most vulnerable to the negative consequences of climate change.

Not only does the burden of climate change disproportionately fall on the world's most vulnerable, but also climate change will increase their susceptibility to all kinds of unpredictable events. Climate change, extreme events such as hurricanes and tsunamis, and sea level rise all contribute to reduced availability of agricultural and natural resources, increased water stress, and greater disease prevalence. This threatens the world's most vulnerable people's livelihoods, health, security, and ability to recover from future shocks — as a result, making them increasingly exposed to hardship.

Since 2008, an annual average of 21.5 million people have been displaced by the floods, storms, wildfires, and extreme temperatures that are increasing in prevalence as a result of climate change, contributing to the global refugee crisis.

It's no wonder that nearly half of millennials believe that climate change is the world's most critical problem, according to a survey by *Business Insider*. The state of the planet impacts nearly every other problem currently facing the world, from food and water security and poverty to inequality and global conflict.

Amid the climate crisis, former Vice President Al Gore contends that there is a need for both urgency and hope.

"After the final no there comes a yes / And on that yes the

future world depends," said Vice President Gore at a keynote address on "The Climate Crisis and Its Solutions," quoting a poem by Wallace Stevens.

In the face of the daunting threats currently facing the planet, Vice President Gore asserts, "A final no followed by a yes — we must, we can, and we will change."

Walking is a promising vehicle for change. Although it does leave literal footprints, walking minimizes your ecological footprint and permits you to develop a closer relationship with your environment in the process. While we often take for granted the beautiful landscapes and scenery that are endangered by climate change, walking permits you to enjoy the beauty of nature in all its glory.

THE NATURAL CHOICE

"Why would we walk for an hour when we could take a 15-minute cab ride that would cost almost nothing?"

I chuckle at my dad's question, until I realize that he isn't kidding.

"The sun is shining and the weather is glorious," I begin, taking his rhetorical question seriously. Hoping to guilt him into walking with me and also enlighten him about the obvious superiority of walking, I rattle off a few other benefits of walking: "It will help you think more clearly... We could always use some more exercise... The time walking is more time that we get to spend together... We won't be responsible for any harmful emissions... You might notice some unexpected things along the way that we definitely wouldn't get to see in a car..."

"That's hard to argue with," he concedes.

To me, walking is the natural choice.

While many people wonder, "Why walk when you could drive?" my personal philosophy is the opposite: "Why drive when you could walk?"

The former philosophy is more dominant than you might imagine. About 70 percent of all car trips in the United States are less than two miles — a perfectly walkable distance. Car trips of less than a mile account for more than 10 billion miles traveled per year. On foot, the average person could travel this same distance in a mere 15 minutes.

"If we all chose to power half of those [less than one mile] trips with our feet instead of petroleum, assuming an average fuel economy of 22 mpg and an average fuel price of $2.50/gallon, we would save about $575 million in fuel costs and about two million metric tons of CO_2 emissions per year," the

Environmental Protection Agency asserts. "That's like taking 400,000 cars off the road each year."

Even though the saved car emissions from any one walking trip are not enough to move the needle on climate change, the collective impact of individuals' decisions over time has the power to create a tangible change — especially in cities overtaken by smog and other visible signs of pollution.

While traveling by foot isn't always possible, I take advantage of the opportunity to walk whenever I can, and I try to encourage my friends and family to do the same.

* * *

On this particular day, I've planned an excursion to the southernmost edge of the Cap d'Antibes peninsula in the south of France. According to the tourism website, the walking route should take approximately two hours to complete in its entirety.

It's my last spring break of college, and my parents, my high school friend Lisa, and I all are spending the week in the charming town of Antibes, France, on the Mediterranean Sea. In the small city, the rust-colored roofs and sand-tinted building exteriors are juxtaposed against the deep azure water and the dazzling cotton candy sky, making it seem as though this wonderland was pulled straight out of a fairytale.

According to Google Maps, it takes about an hour to walk from the city of Antibes to the trail on the adjacent peninsula. I've already convinced my dad that walking is the superior mode of transportation. However, as we leave our rental apartment and walk past a line of taxis on one of the city's outer streets, my mom asks if we can drive to our destination instead.

"It's only a 15-minute journey and would cost hardly anything," she argues.

I insist that we walk, again rattling off my go-to list of the benefits of walking.

The walk is two miles of relatively flat, winding roads, with the Mediterranean Sea to our left and artfully constructed Mediterranean mansions — many blocked from wandering eyes by fences and gates — to our right. With the beauty of nature on one side and man-made marvels on the other, the journey is a feast for the senses. While at first I find myself most intrigued by the expansive houses, the longer we walk, the more I become fascinated by the water. I am enamored by the way the sun's rays hit the surface of the water, causing the sea to twinkle and take on a life of its own.

Our concentration on the landscape is broken as motorcycles and sports cars zip past us. We stay glued to the sidewalk, marveling at the speed with which the vehicles maneuver the sharp turns. I doubt that the people traveling in motorized vehicles are experiencing the Mediterranean's beauty in the same way that we are. If we had taken the taxi as my parents had suggested, we wouldn't have been able to smell the crisp air of the Mediterranean or feel the sun beating down on our skin or hear the sound of waves crashing against the rocky coast in the same way.

In a car, our sensory feast would have become a fleeting snapshot captured by only our eyes.

The longer we walk, the more relaxed I feel. I can sense myself beginning to breathe easier, and my conversation with Lisa flows naturally as our Adidas-clad feet walk in unison. My parents trail behind us, out of earshot but only by a short distance. As I glance back, I see that they, too, are talking and laughing, and I am glad to see that they appear to be enjoying the journey.

After our hour-long excursion, we finally arrive at our destination: *La Plage de la Garoupe.* We are traveling in March, which is quite apparently a part of the off-season for this little beach town. Where there should be tourists lining the pristine beach as in the May to September peak season, only two bold speedo-clad swimmers elect to brave the 50-degree weather. The waterfront's lone open restaurant has a wait time of more than an hour — it's a good thing we packed snacks!

Up until this point, we have encountered only a handful of fellow pedestrians, but now we see a few groups of people converging around the entrance to the waterfront trail. We follow them towards a tree-lined path.

After only a few minutes on the trail, I find that the online literature, which had characterized this hike as "easy," had entirely glossed over the fact that this path is relatively strenuous. The first half-mile of the trail is primarily flat, luring hikers into a false sense of security. Soon, however, the path turns into rocky stairs, leading walkers up 10 steps here, down seven steps there, and then up another 20 steps, with the unpredictable pattern continuing along the rocky coastline. In most places, a rope separates the path on the edge of the cliff from the water below. In other places, it's best not to look down.

"Isn't it beautiful?" I marvel, turning around in order to share my observation with Lisa on the path behind me and my parents a few steps farther behind her.

"I'm too busy trying not to fall off of the rocks to focus on the view!" my mom yells back.

* * *

During the hike, our group stops at one of the many rocky overlooks jutting out from the coast, apparently set aside with the express purpose of reminding the focused hiker to take time to enjoy the view. As I look out at the Mediterranean, I am in awe of how the water seems to go on forever. Only a few white sailboats in the distance interrupt the twinkling blue expanse.

Turning around and looking back at the coast, I find that the rocks form a masterpiece all their own, with stones and boulders in different shades of gray and of a wide variety of sizes stacked upon each other, demonstrating the work of thousands of years of sculpting by wind and rain.

"This is nature's cathedral!" my dad exclaims, interrupting our awe-stricken silence.

Many of the words we use to describe nature — cathedral, masterpiece, and work of art, to name a few — are comparisons to man-made objects. This may be because the only way we could possibly attempt to describe and encapsulate our experience of the utterly indescribable is through man-made comparisons.

On our trip, we've spent a significant amount of time exploring France's ornate cathedrals and churches, captivated by the gold-lined altars, seemingly unfathomable architectural feats, and carefully painted holy icons. These buildings showcase the very best of human craftsmanship, attempting to bridge the gap between the human and the divine, and walking through them provides an opportunity to reflect in silence.

In the same way that those cathedrals bear the mark of human influence, nature is shaped by the actions of mankind. From oil spills, greenhouse gas emissions, and litter, to human efforts to protect the natural landscape, humans exert their influence on the natural world in both good ways and bad. The tangible evidence of this interaction manifests itself in many ways, from melting glaciers to rising sea levels to changing global temperatures.

Moving quickly along a coastline in a motorized vehicle, it's easy to glimpse only the beauty of the landscape and to forget about its imperfections and the threats to its sustained future functioning. As I hike on foot, however, I am forced to face the paper remnants of someone's lunch picnic washed up on the shore and the broken glass beer bottle from another's presumed late-night shenanigans on the trail.

The path itself is manmade. Still, it's constructed in a primitive kind of way that is just sturdy enough for people to traverse safely while still permitting a deeper level of engagement with the natural environment. In certain places, the flat stone path and stepped rocks give way to free-form rocks with only sporadic pieces of blue tape to indicate that we are still following the correct path.

"Why didn't you tell us to wear hiking shoes?" I hear Lisa say behind me, interrupting my thoughts as I navigate the rocky path.

"I didn't know it would be so rocky!" I yell back, becoming aware of the feeling of the pointed rocks indenting the soles of my own shoes.

This interaction of rubber shoe soles and rocks serves as a reminder that the experience of nature in the form of a hike is far removed from the rhythm of daily life. Indeed, encountering nature requires a degree of preparation. Sunscreen or other sun protection is a useful addition to any hike, as I discovered when I woke up the day following our adventure with a bright red nose and chest. Likewise, water and food are eventually required to sustain any outdoor experience. As we learned about our unsuitable apparel, footwear and proper attire are also necessary prerequisites for many natural experiences.

Anyone walking to change the world must be prepared to bring their best self into nature's cathedral, in order to make room for what might be discovered.

✳ ✳ ✳

"I'm usually not a huge walker, but I had a lot of fun," Lisa says as we climb the stairs up to our apartment at the conclusion of our journey.

Despite our lack of complete preparation for the relatively intense natural experience — and perhaps even because of it — she adds, "I feel more connected to nature after going for that long walk."

As proof, she can still feel the pangs of the rocks on her feet.

My parents lag a few steps behind us on the stairs, but my mom interjects, "I'd like to request that you do more research before taking us on a hike again in the future." After a pause, she adds, "But overall, I enjoyed getting out of the city, taking in the beautiful views, and, of course, spending time with you all."

I smile, glad to know that they don't resent me for dragging them on what turned out to be an all-day walking excursion.

For me, it was a welcome experience to enjoy the beauty of nature in one of the most remote locations I have ever visited. I felt a sense of freedom and clarity of mind that I rarely find in the concrete jungle.

When learning about climate change and other threats to the environment, I easily feel overwhelmed and powerless in the face of seemingly irreversible destruction. Natural encounters have taught me that when the world appears to be falling apart, it is essential to cherish the joy of living in the present and to wholeheartedly embrace the beauty of the very thing you are trying to preserve.

WALK THE EARTH

The slick oil floated to the surface of the once-blue water as oil-covered animals lay dead or struggling to live, the air thick with the overwhelming smell of rotten eggs.

Nothing about the San Francisco Bay in the aftermath of the 1971 oil spill was beautiful.

Living adjacent to the San Francisco Bay in Marin County, John Francis witnessed the impact of the oil spill firsthand. The 20-year-old son of working-class African-American parents from Philadelphia, he had moved to California two years prior to the spill. In the immediate aftermath of the oil spill, Dr. Francis was moved to action, helping clean the beaches and save the local wildlife. As someone who regularly used oil products, especially to fuel his car, he felt personally responsible for the oil spill.

"I never want to ride in a car again," he said in jest to a friend after witnessing the spill's devastating effects.

As time passed, Dr. Francis felt a growing desire to make a

deeper commitment to his environmental preservation efforts. He decided to stop using motorized vehicles entirely.

Walking would be his only mode of transportation.

He thought that when he started walking everyone else who had witnessed the extreme environmental degradation would follow. Instead, his radical decision was met with controversy, criticism, and contempt.

"Life is hard enough for a black man. Why would you tie a rock around your neck?" one critic said.

It didn't take long for Dr. Francis to become frustrated by the time he spent arguing with friends, family, acquaintances, and strangers about the oil spill and his decision to take up walking as his only form of transportation. Shortly after deciding to stop using motorized vehicles, Dr. Francis made another radical decision: to stop speaking.

At first, he committed to a singular day of silence. One day turned into two days, which turned into a week, which turned into a year, which turned into a full 17 years of silence. While his silence was initially intended as a gift for his community to not have to listen to him arguing about the oil spill all of the time, Dr. Francis quickly discovered that refraining from talking actually had the effect of enhancing his ability to drive environmental impact.

Environmental activists tend to "shout [their] message from the rooftops," Dr. Francis noted in an interview with *The Atlantic*. His decision to protest by silently walking was contradictory to what was expected from environmental activists. His silence and his footsteps spoke louder than words.

Dr. Francis' decisions drastically slowed the pace of his life. Whereas he was once able to express himself simply and straightforwardly through words, it took time for him to get his point across through sign language and hand motions. While motor vehicles allowed Dr. Francis to quickly transport himself from one point to another, relying on his feet for transportation required a greater degree of planning in order to allot enough time to travel a distance that used to be covered in a quick car ride.

Although his transportation and conversations were indeed more slowly paced, Dr. Francis' commitment to walking and silence did not inhibit his ability to successfully move forward in his education and career. Dr. Francis' journey actually gave him the credibility necessary to be an effective environmental activist. Soon after making the decision to walk, he hiked 500 miles north to Southern Oregon University, where he received his Bachelor of Science degree. Next, he trekked to the University of Montana-Missoula to pursue a Master's degree in

Environmental Studies, followed by a Ph.D. in Land Resources from the Gaylord Nelson Institute for Environmental Studies at the University of Wisconsin-Madison.

By moving at a human speed — as opposed to driving or biking — Dr. Francis experienced the places he walked at a deeper level, taking the time to notice both the beautiful and damaged aspects of the landscape. Walking primarily along America's highways, Dr. Francis witnessed everything from majestic forests and litter to rolling fields and roadkill.

While walking across the United States, he adopted the practice of taking transects of the natural environment. Transect walks are a popular technique for community observation and improvement that can be done by anyone. On a transect walk, you investigate the natural, built, and experienced environments with the goal of addressing a specific issue (such as access to food or water) or of conducting a general audit to learn about local behaviors and needs. By counting and recording the occurrence of the chosen object of study along the designated path of observation, transect walk participants develop greater environmental awareness and appreciation.

Dr. Francis' close observation of the environment during his walking journey better prepared him to defend it.

✳ ✳ ✳

When the Exxon Valdez oil spill occurred in March 1989, Dr. Francis was actively researching oil spill management at the University of Wisconsin-Madison Nelson Institute, making him one of the most educated people on the subject at the time. His years of walking activism and his educational background prepared him to take on a role as project manager for the United States Coast Guard Oil Pollution Act Staff, writing oil spill regulations.

In order to excel in his new position, Dr. Francis realized that he would need to break his 17 years of silence. Despite starting to talk again, he maintained his commitment to walking, traveling by foot from the University of Wisconsin to the office in the nation's capital to begin his new position.

In total, it took him seven years and a day to walk across the United States.

In his TED Talk, "Walk the Earth…," Dr. Francis jokes:

"Twenty years ago, if someone had said to me, 'John, do you really want to make a difference?'

'Yeah, I want to make a difference.'

He said, 'You just start walking east; get out of your car and just start walking east.'

And as I walked off a little bit, they'd say, 'Yeah, and shut up, too.'"

Despite the impact of his years of walking, Dr. Francis began to realize that his commitment to walking was actually inhibiting his ability to effectively advance his mission as an environmental activist. On one particular occasion in his role as an Ambassador to the United Nations in 1994, he had to take a sailboat and walk to Venezuela in order to share his message of environmental awareness on a broader scale.

"It took me 100 miles to figure out that I had become a prisoner... The prison that I was in was the fact that I did not drive or use motorized vehicles," Dr. Francis reflected on his international walking experience in Venezuela. "I was so used to the guy who only just walked. I didn't know who I would be if I changed."

When he first committed to not using motor vehicle transportation, Dr. Francis never imagined that he would have a Ph.D. or become a U.N. Ambassador. During his many years of walking, he had never thought twice about his decision. In order to ensure that he was engaged in the practice for the right reasons and to maximize his personal impact, Dr. Francis realized that it was important to constantly reevaluate his commitment to walking given new knowledge and information.

"I had a responsibility to more than just me," Dr. Francis recognized upon reflection.

Stepping onto a bus at the border of Venezuela and Brazil, he gained the courage to move into the next phase of his work as an environmental activist.

After the short bus ride, he took a plane back to the United States. Within five minutes of traveling in the plane from Caracas, Dr. Francis realized that he was flying over Puerto Rico. After 22 years without using motorized vehicles, he was moved to tears: it had taken him more than a month to cover that same distance by boat and foot.

* * *

It's easy to lose sight of the "miracle of modern transportation" when it is such a normalized part of daily life, Dr. Francis believes. He encourages all of us to take the time to marvel at the genius of modern technology.

Although automobiles are traditionally symbolic of freedom, Dr. Francis found that walking gave him more personal freedom than any other form of transportation. When Dr. Francis had access to an automobile, he could easily travel whenever he wanted anywhere he wanted within a broad radius.

Walking required Dr. Francis to move at a slower pace than any other mode of transportation. Relying solely on his feet for transportation required a greater degree of planning, significantly reducing the size of the circle in which he could operate on a daily basis. As a result, Dr. Francis had to be intentional about everything he did and everywhere he went. Walking afforded him the opportunity to be truly present in his environment.

This attitude of intentionality serves as an example to all travelers, regardless of the transportation mode. If everyone who drove a motorized vehicle adopted an attitude of intentional movement each time he or she sat down in a car — considering the necessity of the journey in the first place and weighing the possibility of walking instead of driving — one can only imagine the positive environmental impact that would result. This attitude shift surely would make a dent in the Environmental Protection Agency's goal of reducing by half all car trips of less than a mile.

Dr. Francis recognizes that relying on walking as one's only form of transportation is a radical decision that is simply not possible for the large majority of the population. Being mindful about your transportation decisions is an accessible way to reduce your environmental footprint, choosing to walk whenever possible and eliminating unnecessary automobile journeys.

* * *

Although walking was the initial tool for amplifying his message, walking greatly reduced Dr. Francis' potential sphere of impact. Now, he realizes that it would be impossible to balance working, spending time with his family, and traveling as an activist without taking advantage of transportation technology.

While he no longer relies on walking as his only form of transportation, Dr. Francis has by no means stopped walking. He still strives to walk at least four miles per day and takes an annual walking journey of approximately 100 miles across the United States.

Dr. Francis believes that more people should have access to these kinds of natural experiences. Many Americans drive through stretches of the country and recognize the beauty of the countryside without ever taking the time to stop and encounter it in a personal way, he notes. Walking in nature provides a gateway into understanding the natural world, engaging in other natural experiences, and making environmentally responsible decisions in the future.

Through his nonprofit, Planetwalk, Dr. Francis provides diverse groups of people with the opportunity to walk in nature through concentrated experiences of life as a Planetwalker. For a week at a time, he takes groups on walks that range from five to 20 miles per day. Participants range in age from 11 to 82 years old, hail from all around the country, and have opportunities to receive financial aid to finance the journey. Through efforts such as this, walking in nature can be accessible to people regardless of their age or other demographic factors.

People, after all, are an essential component of the environment, Dr. Francis reminds us.

In 2005, Dr. Francis embarked on a journey to retrace his original route across the United States with the goal of studying how the landscape had changed as well as redefining environmental priorities.

His primary finding: "People are part of the environment."

"Our first opportunity to treat the environment sustainably, or even understand what sustainability is, can be found in our relationships with ourselves and each other," he said in an interview with *The Atlantic*. "So this is definitely a change of consciousness and practice that will allow us to address the great environmental difficulties that we face. It may come simply from each person's heart. The environment is therefore also about human rights, civil rights, gender equality, economic and education equity."

There must be a social dimension to the environmental movement in order to collaboratively work to confront the daunting environmental challenges we face.

And what better way to begin than by walking together?

As you may have guessed, walking for environmental impact isn't quite that simple. As you'll soon learn, safety threats and systemic factors jeopardize people's ability to walk, leaving many with no choice other than to rely on a transportation mode with a high environmental footprint.

THE FOOTPRINT(S) WE LEAVE

Like Dr. Francis, Sarah Stiles, a sociology professor at Georgetown University, came of age during an oil crisis: the Arab Oil Embargo. At the time, it was considered more of an ethical than an environmental issue to conserve energy. When the Organization of the Petroleum Exporting Countries (OPEC) stopped shipping oil to the United States and other countries backing Israel in the Yom Kippur War, each individual was expected to do their part in confronting the national crisis.

The United States government responded to the oil embargo by deregulating natural gas prices, expanding domestic energy production, and promoting energy conservation. Along with these measures, it was considered an individual responsibility to conserve energy in whatever ways possible. One of the ways to contribute was — you guessed it — walking.

While the motivation for conserving energy was primarily security-based, the oil crisis was a blessing in disguise. It "inadvertently gave the rest of the world a life-saving head start in the struggle to avoid, or at least mitigate, the threat of catastrophic climate change," according to *Foreign Affairs*.

Growing up in Dallas, Texas, where car culture dominated, Professor Stiles found it difficult to transport by any method other than motor vehicle in the sprawling metropolitan region. Since walking and biking weren't in the realm of possibility, her family reduced their automobile energy use by taking car trips only when it was absolutely necessary. Still, it required a considerable amount of fuel to drive to work, school, the grocery store, and other essential locations.

When she moved to Boston to complete her master's degree, Professor Stiles was able to formally commit to transporting only by walking and biking, pledging to stop using cars altogether. While it felt like a natural choice to Professor Stiles, her decision not to own or operate a car encountered controversy.

"You're riding a bike because you can't afford a car!" one man shouted at her from a car while she was biking in Boston. He didn't understand that her decision was for moral rather than financial reasons — although the low cost of transport was a welcome benefit of her decision.

"Look at all of the tons of carbon I haven't emitted!" she wanted to respond.

Ultimately, Professor Stiles stopped biking in cities because of the danger posed by the transportation method.

"I don't have time to get hit by someone selfishly driving a car distracted," she says.

She still walks because she feels more in control of her safety in the face of unpredictable automobile operators than she does when biking, although there are safety risks posed by both walking and biking.

In 2016, more than 6,000 pedestrians and over 800 bicyclists were killed in the United States alone. Reaching a 25-year high, these deaths accounted for nearly 20 percent of total U.S. fatalities that year. In a world dominated by motor vehicles, walking and biking are inherently dangerous modes of transportation.

To improve safety in the short-term, the National Highway Traffic Safety Administration suggests that pedestrians use sidewalks, avoid unpredictable walking behavior, cross at crosswalks, and try to make eye contact when passing in front of drivers. In order to ensure long-term pedestrian safety, the Center for American Progress proposes promoting pedestrian-friendly design and embracing principles of smart growth. Centering design around people rather than cars, smart growth cities rely more on mass transit and are more compact, with more essential services located within shorter, walkable distances.

Since people are a critical component of the environment, making the world safer for pedestrians is a first step towards enhanced environmental wellbeing.

* * *

Designing sustainable cities around walkability takes for granted that walking is actually better for the environment than automobile transport.

How can we be sure that walking is in reality the form of transportation with the lower environmental footprint?

Economics professor Richard Mckenzie calls into question the very principle that walking is better for the environment than driving a car. Backed by an extensive analysis of food supply chain carbon emissions, he argues that driving is better for the planet than walking. After all, calories burned by walking must be replenished by food, which results in the waste of the fossil fuels and greenhouse gases that are inherent to the food production and transportation supply chain.

Professor Mckenzie raises a valid point, but he fails to take into account a few important details.

The Pacific Institute, an environmental research organization, was determined to disprove Professor Mckenzie's counterintuitive assertion. The Institute found that walking is only worse for the environment than driving in the case that a person is consuming a diet composed entirely of greenhouse-gas intensive food such as beef. Although the average American diet — stereotypically known for its fast-food burgers — is more energy-intensive than in many other countries, it has a considerable variety beyond only the most greenhouse-gas intensive foods. In reality, Americans eat a greater variety of less greenhouse-gas intensive foods, such as fruits and vegetables, than Professor Mckenzie accounts for. When considering the average American diet, "walking 1.5 miles would generate less than a quarter of the GHG that would be emitted if the person drove the same distance," according to research by the Center for American Progress.

Professor Mckenzie's argument also doesn't consider the many environmental benefits of walking that go beyond greenhouse-gas emissions. Walking reduces traffic congestion, air and noise pollution, the destruction of open space, and auto-related accidents and deaths — all of which positively benefit the environment and society.

As someone who has been walking under the assumption that it is the environmentally favorable option, the Pacific Institute's research was a source of great relief.

Every day, you have the power to reduce your personal environmental footprint through your choice of transportation mode. As Professor Stiles discovered growing up in Dallas, however, walking isn't always a feasible option. Improving pedestrian safety and designing cities with pedestrians in mind are two ways to reduce harmful environmental footprints through walkability.

Walking is a way to make a mark on your environment without leaving the harm characteristic of other transportation modes. Still, there are forces that block the ability to walk and contribute to its environmental benefits.

TAKE A HIKE

"Why not walk?" I asked.

"I didn't see the point."

On an uncharacteristically warm and sunny February day in Washington, D.C., Lara Fishbane and I sat and chatted at an outdoor table on Georgetown University's campus. While I indeed appreciated the pleasant weather, I worried about its environmental implications. Only a few years ago, we would have been anticipating a snowstorm around this time of year.

Our outdoor conversation was a welcome break from our workday at the Beeck Center for Social Impact and Innovation on Georgetown's campus, where Lara was a research associate and I worked as a student analyst.

Lara grew up in a New York suburb, where she could simply hop in a car and easily travel from one point to another. On top of participating in other physical activities such as gymnastics and basketball, she didn't feel the need to unnecessarily exert energy to walk any further than was absolutely necessary — in her case, the distance between the car and the door. While Lara's mom always enjoyed walking and hiking, Lara thought it was particularly strange when her mom would suggest walking the mile from her house to the local bank.

"Walking felt like effort," Lara recounted.

Now an outdoor enthusiast, Lara has become an avid hiker.

What changed?

When Lara came to Washington, D.C., for college, she found herself walking frequently around Georgetown University's campus and the rest of the city. Although she enjoyed exploring the city on foot, she felt constrained by the buildings towering above her. It was a stressful experience to be surrounded by so many other pedestrians — not to mention bikes, cars, and buses — all in a rush to get somewhere.

"I forgot that I was part of something bigger," Lara reflected.

As a result, Lara turned to hiking. Throughout college, she explored the trails around Washington, D.C. — from the Billy Goat Trail in Maryland to more adventurous treks in Shenandoah, Virginia. Experiencing nature by hiking provided Lara with the chance to see expansive natural landscapes that she could not have encountered when walking through the city blocks.

When walking on the streets of a city, Lara's vision became limited to the immediate block where she was walking. With a smaller field of vision, she found that it was easy to become limited in her thinking and to consider only the smaller picture of her immediate circumstances.

When hiking in the great outdoors, Lara felt humbled to be able to look out and see places and people that were far away from her own reach.

"There's so much that I don't understand about the environment," Lara realized.

Experiencing nature firsthand inspired her to learn more about the environment and how she fit into it, as well as to seek out more natural experiences.

Annually, Lara participates in the Sierra Club's One Day Hike. As the name suggests, hikers travel in one day the 62.14 miles from the Thompson Boat Center in Georgetown, D.C., to the Bolivar Community Center in Harpers Ferry, West Virginia, along the C&O Canal towpath. Starting at the absurdly early hour of 3:00 am and ending just before midnight, the hike leads participants through urban, suburban, and rural areas. The grueling journey literally connects the city with its suburbs and rural regions, clearly demonstrating their interconnectedness.

Before she started hiking, Lara viewed urban and rural areas as completely distinct realms. Walking through both the city and country reminded Lara that actions taken in both realms had interwoven consequences on the environment as a whole.

This simultaneously paralyzing and action-inspiring realization motivates Lara to continue exploring the world on foot.

* * *

Not only does hiking provide access to fresh air, beautiful views, and all that nature has to offer, but also it increases calorie burn and tones a different set of muscles compared with simply walking. According to the Stanford University study mentioned in Step 2, hiking in nature also reduces the mind's propensity to ruminate, or develop negative, self-focused thought patterns linked with anxiety and depression.

Hiking is a way to walk towards a happy and healthy life in relationship with yourself, others, and the natural environment. Still, the overwhelming benefits of hiking are not accessible to everyone.

While Lara enjoys hiking and its many benefits, she recognizes that hiking is an inherently privileged way to walk. Although programs such as John Francis' Planetwalk strive to be accessible to people regardless of their backgrounds, many natural experiences — and their accompanying benefits — remain broadly inaccessible with many barriers to entry.

"Unlike going to the movies, eating at a restaurant, or other 'luxuries,' spending time in nature seems free. But not everyone has equal access," warns Emily Zak in her *Everyday Feminism* article, "Outdoor Recreation Isn't Free — Why We Need to Stop Pretending It Is."

Many hikes require that a participant first travel to the hike's location. On top of that, there are certain societal standards of how one is expected to dress for hiking. Obtaining the necessary equipment and attire may prove to be too expensive or not worth the trouble for many people. For those pursuing overnight adventures or longer hikes such as the Appalachian Trail, the costs add up quickly: gear, insurance, food, accommodations, gear replacement for long-term hikers, and the opportunity costs associated with being away from home and work. The price tag for just food, accommodation, and gear runs upwards of $1,000 per month on the Appalachian Trail.

Beyond cost, hiking is inherently inaccessible to people with disabilities. Many hiking trails involve steep inclines and rocky paths, which present a challenge for people with disabilities of any kind, especially for those in wheelchairs.

Professor Stiles is particularly cognizant of the inaccessibility of hiking, as her friend Nancy is paraplegic. While Professor Stiles and her friends have always enjoyed hiking together, they wanted to be able to plan activities that were inclusive of Nancy. As a result, they researched wheelchair-accessible trails and found a multitude of hiking trails that are safe for people with special mobility needs. Websites such as Trail Link and American Trails list a geographically diverse variety of accessible trails in each of the 50 states and the District of Columbia. While hiking trails will never be perfectly accessible, the number of wheelchair-friendly trails across the United

States is steadily increasing, providing the opportunity for a greater variety of people to closely experience nature.

Aside from cost and physical ability, there are longstanding, systematically reinforced stereotypes about who can and cannot hike. While national parks and hiking trails are viewed by many as untouched wilderness, there is a much more complicated history behind the parks.

"Many national parks and public lands were built on colonized lands," Emily Zak notes. "Even U.S. National Parks reflect colonialism, where white leaders ignored Indigenous people in the area to establish [the parks]."

With the media's representation of hiking historically primarily portraying able-bodied white men, many minorities feel that hiking is not intended for them. National park attendance rates reflect this notion: 80 percent of national park visitors and 75 percent of young adults participating in outdoor activities in the United States in 2016 were white.

Try typing the word "hiking" into the "Images" tab of a search engine. I had to press the "show more results" button at the bottom of the page two times before finding a picture including a person of color among all of the picturesque images of backpack-clad hikers posing atop mountains or walking along wooded trails.

"It's hard to see yourself in the outdoor community if you don't physically see others like you," Ambreen Tariq told *Outside*. A Muslim woman of color and immigrant, Ambreen runs Brown People Camping, a social media initiative to promote diversity in public lands. In the face of lore about Daniel Boone and other great American outdoorsmen, she didn't have a family tradition of outdoor exploration to fall back on.

"Not only did I not have an authentic background doing activities in the outdoors, but my family didn't do it, and I don't have the legacy of being connected to a piece of land because we were always moving," she said in the *Outside* article. As a result, Tariq believes in the value of sharing her outdoor experiences in order to encourage more people to embrace the outdoors.

In addition to Brown People Camping, campaigns such as the Fresh Air Fund, Vida Verde, Outdoor Afro, and Latino Outdoors have all contributed to making outdoor experiences more accessible to people regardless of their race, ethnicity, gender, or socio-economic status.

When it comes to building an inclusive environmental movement, Ambreen Tariq says it best: "The more of us who can connect to it, the more we can protect it together."

In this way, a powerful first step in promoting environmental wellbeing is ensuring that no one feels like an outsider in the outdoors.

———

In confronting the global environmental crisis, walking is a vehicle for minimizing harmful emissions, understanding the environment, and advocating for environmental preservation. Catalyzing the kind of change capable of moving the needle on climate change will require a societal shift towards environmental stewardship that affords all people the opportunity to walk in nature. Together, our steps have the power to change our environmental footprint from one of pollution and destruction to one of respect and conservation.

STEP 8.

THE WALKING ECONOMY

———

Until the early 20th century, American cities were designed for pedestrians.

Then, the invention of the automobile changed everything.

Before the automobile, people either lived and worked in the city or lived and worked on a farm in the countryside. Essentially everything required to live — employment, food, friends and family — was located within walking distance.

The University of Colorado Boulder's "History of the Automobile" shows just how much society's living patterns changed in a matter of decades. Beginning in the 1910s, automobiles began to dominate American streets, providing car owners with a previously unprecedented level of geographic flexibility. During World War II, a shortage of motors, fuel, and tires led to low automobile availability and a brief shift towards mass transit.

When was the war was over, the Golden Age of the Automobile began. A post-war excess of the same supplies required to manufacture and operate cars led the U.S. to become a car-producing machine. In this post-war era, Americans reveled in the freedom and flexibility provided by the automobile. By the late 1940s and early 1950s, society had become automobile-oriented, ringing in the era of interstate highways, fast food restaurants, gas stations, and convenience stores. The Automobile Age benefitted the economy by creating jobs in automobile-driven industries, from steel production and automobile assembly to drive-in movies and drive-through banks. The automobile drove the growth of the suburban economy and enabled people to travel longer distances to work.

Despite the undeniable benefits of the automobile, its convenience threatened a lifestyle wherein people primarily moved around on foot. The automobile made it possible for people to travel from home, to work or school, to running errands, and back home, all while walking only the distance from a parking spot to the door of the destination. This new pattern of transportation greatly minimized the ability of individuals to interact with their surrounding communities in a meaningful way. The automobile, the suburbs, and the network of highways all worked together to fundamentally change society's transportation patterns.

Now, all signs point to walking as the driver of economic growth. Centering the economy around walking has the power to boost economic performance and, in the process, make all of society better off. Making the walking economy a reality will require the collaborative planning and support of all of the people responsible for shaping a place.

THE COMEBACK KID

Despite the historic shift away from walkability in favor of the automobile, walking is making a comeback.

Adam Ducker, who has been practicing real estate for more than two decades, has directly observed the resurgence in the popularity of walking. People are rediscovering the joys of living in a concentrated geographical area, especially the ability to walk to work, school, food and other retailers, and recreational activities. Compared to an automobile commute, walking is a healthier, less stressful alternative that allows you to see the sights, interact with fellow pedestrians, and enjoy yourself while on the way to your final destination.

As a Managing Director at the Robert Charles Lesser & Co. (RCLCO) real estate advisory firm, Adam has experienced firsthand the shift in the real estate market in favor of walkability. All else equal, walkability in and of itself is a factor that leads to price premiums by residential buyers. The allure of "being within walking distance" of work, schools, stores, and more has led to an explosion of demand for walkability and, as a result, increased prices for homes in walkable areas. CEOs for Cities, a non-profit that shares best practices for economic success in U.S. cities, identifies walking as a key best practice. According to a 2009 CEOs for Cities study, "houses located in areas with above-average walkability or bike-ability are worth up to $34,000 more than similar houses in areas with average walkability levels."

To Adam, the Atlanta BeltLine is a prime example of the walking economy in action. Expanding upon Atlanta's existing streetcar system, the BeltLine is a 22-mile modern streetcar network accompanied by 33 miles of multi-purpose trails and 2,000 acres of parks. These trails connect 45 Atlanta neighborhoods, bridging the divide among people and communities that were previously separated — both literally and figuratively.

"[Atlanta] residents have a tendency to think of themselves as living in one of four quadrants: the prosperous and bustling Northeast, the quirky and hip Southeast, the overlooked but culturally vibrant Southwest and the bleak but rapidly redeveloping Northwest," according to Rebecca Serna of the Rails to Trails Conservancy. Along with these perceived differences, the neighborhoods were literally separated by highways and urban renewal projects. The BeltLine not only connects the communities but also provides a shared space for members of the four distinct neighborhoods to interact and walk together, blurring the lines that used to separate the regions of the city.

The BeltLine innovatively utilizes the remnants of Atlanta's industrial boom, transforming unused properties into public spaces that are accessible to people of all income levels. This project honors Atlanta's industrial history, while also creating value from a previously-wasted resource and setting the city up for a walkable future.

As a city, Atlanta is an early adopter of walkability in the United States. The BeltLine project plays on Atlanta residents' demonstrated desire to live in a connected, walkable community, and it promotes equal access to experience this opportunity by developing affordable housing along the trail system. The project — still a work in progress with expected completion in 2030 — has already yielded an eight-to-one return on investment by promoting $3.7 billion in economic development. Through its job creation potential and its revitalization of the city of Atlanta, the BeltLine is estimated to drive $10 to $20 billion in economic growth by the project's completion.

What has been the key to the BeltLine's success so far?

Collaboration.

The project would not exist without the collaborative funding and support of the government, foundations, and private enterprise. Feedback from Atlanta citizens from all four quadrants has also been critical in planning and executing the project. All parties involved recognize the potential for the BeltLine to boost the economy and enhance the city's quality of life. The project's demonstrated success thus far is attracting even more contributions from all sectors.

By embracing Atlanta's industrial past and reinvigorating the city for future growth, the Atlanta BeltLine demonstrates the success of a multi-stakeholder project with walkability at its core. Although the BeltLine provides a model for successfully implementing walkability in urban areas, suburban and rural areas present different challenges. Still, these smaller communities are demonstrating their ability to innovate for walkable futures.

∗ ∗ ∗

While discussions of walkability typically revolve around cities, the suburbs are gaining new momentum around walkability.

"Suburban areas are some of the hardest places to create walking opportunities," Adam acknowledges.

When it comes to implementing walkability in urban areas, it typically involves improving the city's existing resources, whether it is lighting, sidewalk cleanliness, or public spaces such as parks. Meanwhile, suburbs have little to no existing walking infrastructure in place due to the dependency on cars inherent to suburbia.

Despite the more difficult implementation, suburban walkability is a trend that is here to stay.

An overwhelming 50 percent of U.S. residents list walkability as the top priority or as a high priority when considering where to live, according to the Urban Land Institute. As a result, networks of trails and designated suburban "walkable communities" are garnering price premiums. Suburban walking communities positioned around town centers are especially desirable for young homeowners and renters, who deem these places to be "urban light."

"People are very eager to create a life that blends the best features of the American suburb and urbanity," Adam says.

A 2007 RCLCO survey discovered that 43 percent of millennials prefer to live in a "close-in suburb." Compared to the stereotypical American suburb with its big houses, fenced-in yards, and multiple cars per household, a close-in suburb has smaller houses that are closer together, smaller and fewer cars per household, and walkable access to restaurants, stores, parks, and more. This preference for condensed suburbs reflects the millennial generation's priorities of low-cost living, sustainability, community participation, and taking part in the sharing economy, all of which are enhanced through the low physical footprint lifestyles of close-in suburbs.

"The shift away from traditional suburbs toward denser, urban-light living could have major economic-growth implications on its own. Economic research shows that doubling a community's population density tends to increase productivity by anywhere between six percent and 28 percent..." state Derek Thompson and Jordan Weissmann in "The Cheapest Generation," a profile on millennials' buying habits published in *The Atlantic*. "Our wealth, after all, is determined not only by our own skills and talents, but by our ability to access the ideas of those around us; there's a lot to be gained by increasing the odds that smart people might bump against each other."

Suburban walkable communities attain these economic advantages by replicating the benefits of city living on a smaller scale, through suburban town center developments or trails and paths connecting suburban communities to each other. New parks and trails are being developed through both public and private sector efforts, with an increase in property value along the trail in mind.

By 2014, a former golf course in North Little Rock, Arkansas, had become an overgrown eyesore. After the course was donated to the city by its former owners, local government decided to transform the unused land into a suburban park that would benefit the entire community. With a $40,000 investment appropriated by the City Council, the city improved the course's walking paths, stocked the fishing lake, and transformed the pro shop into a community center. The previous cart paths are now ideally suited to their new role as walking trails, and the once-unkempt green space provides an ideal park for pedestrians. According to local realtors, the investment in the community walking space increased local property values and improved quality of life, benefitting the entire community in the process.

* * *

Compared to urban and suburban regions, rural areas are still lagging behind in achieving walkability. Geographically spread-out places and high-speed automobile traffic traveling on poorly lit, narrow roads make pedestrianism in rural regions highly impractical and unsafe. Still, rural communities around the United States are rallying behind walkability, realizing its host of economic and other benefits.

In 2009, Albert Lea, a town of 18,000 residents in southern Minnesota, was facing a crisis. The town — formerly known for its meatpacking — had lost its economic vitality. Sixty percent of the population was overweight and obese. While the town had a lot of potential, it was in desperate need of a makeover.

It was at this point that Victoria Simonsen, Albert Lea's city manager, convinced the Blue Zones team to test its city health makeover initiative in Albert Lea. Blue Zones is an organization dedicated to helping people live longer and healthier lives by replicating the habits of the healthiest and longest-living communities around the world. As part of the Blue Zones initiative, Albert Lea adopted a community-wide commitment to walking and wellness.

The campaign was based on a three-prong strategy. First, in collaboration with local businesses, schools, media, and other organizations, the town launched a public education campaign highlighting the benefits of physical activity. Second, the Blue Zones team applied social theory, organizing people into walking groups to encourage them to walk together regularly. Finally, the town invested in infrastructure, including developing a five-mile trail adjacent to downtown Albert Lea, strategically constructing 6.5 miles of sidewalks near schools, senior centers, and businesses, and making adjustments to improve the walkability of the downtown region.

Approximately 4,500 participants collectively lost four tons of weight in five years. While initially undertaken for health reasons, the initiative resulted in overwhelming economic benefits shared among residents.

"The city's health insurance premiums [did] not increase in 2015, instead of the double digit increases of the [previous] few years," according to City Manager Chad Adams. As a result, taxpayers — both participants and non-participants — directly benefited from lower insurance costs.

Adams also recognizes the importance of developing a walkable community in order to attract businesses and young residents to sustain the town for the future. The shifts to encourage walkability revitalized the downtown, with 15 new businesses opened and property values increasing by $1.2 million between 2013 and 2016. Now, Albert Lea is alive with people regularly walking among the shops, restaurants, churches, library, bank, and other establishments, providing the town with an economic boost through their purchases.

"When I first came into Albert Lea, I'll be honest, it looked like the downtown was closed," reflects Dan Burden, the Director of Innovation and Inspiration at Blue Zones. As an expert on walkable communities, he helped implement Albert Lea's plan of action for walkability. "There were businesses, but there was no life on the streets. That's changed now."

The story of Albert Lea shows that change is possible, even in the face of the many barriers to walkability in rural America. With strategic investment and serious commitment, walkability has the potential to pay dividends for communities of all sizes.

* * *

These stories of urban, suburban, and rural innovation are a source of hope for the future of walkability. Still, walkability is not equally prioritized everywhere.

"In many places, walking is dangerous at best and illegal at worst," Adam says.

Relying on only their own feet, pedestrians are more vulnerable than users of other forms of transportation. They risk getting hit by speeding cars, assaulted by perpetrators, or attacked by animals — a more salient threat in some areas of the world than in others. In other places, pedestrians are legally prevented from walking due to "No Trespassing" signs. In other places still, discriminatory police practices such as stop-and-frisk mean that pedestrians doing nothing other than walking down the street can be stopped and searched by police officers, often as a result of racial profiling.

In order to reap the economic benefits of walking, the transportation mode must be accessible and safe. Adam is a member of the Urban Land Institute (ULI), which aims to confront some of the obstacles to walkability. One of ULI's initiatives is to ensure that all Americans live within a 10-minute walk of a high-quality park or green space. With more than 100 million Americans currently lacking access to a park, this is an ambitious goal to say the least.

Still, the initiative's endorsement by mayors shows that public officials broadly recognize the benefits of walkable spaces. Economically, improving walkability through parks boosts businesses and revitalizes neighborhoods. Building parks provides a quick return on investment, along with the other non-quantifiable benefits of walkability including physical and mental health, community-building, and environmental sustainability.

When it comes to making the 10-minute walk standard a reality, mayors are innovating by changing zoning to encourage park development, prioritizing parks in master planning, and expanding joint use agreements to permit school recreational facilities to be used by the public. Mayors' demonstrated commitment to park access showcases the potential for local-level investments in walkability to drive wide-reaching change. Projects to enhance walkability, such as parks, have the power to transform once worn-down neighborhoods into economically vibrant places.

THE ECONOMICS OF PLACEMAKING

Placemaking — the foundation of an individual's ability to walk for a better world — is critical for maximizing the economic value of investments in walking and walkability.

Although placemaking encompasses more than the physical characteristics of a location, it can be enhanced by creative urban planning. Placemaking — the collaborative process of creating public spaces that are desirable for people to live, work, play, and learn in — encourages people to spend more time in a location, and as a result spend more money.

As you discovered in Step 1, walking is an inherent component of good placemaking. According to Adam, walkability has the potential to change transactional experiences into recreational ones.

To test this theory, I consider the differences in the way I run errands when I am home in suburban Maryland compared to when I am at school in Washington, D.C.

At home, I hop in the car and drive to the CVS about six miles from my house to pick up a prescription. From there, I drive to get lunch at the Chick-Fil-A drive-thru a mile away from CVS. While driving another two miles to Safeway, I pick up chicken nuggets from the box one at a time, careful to keep my eyes on the road. In the parking lot, I try to park at one of the farther stops from Safeway's sliding glass doors in order to get my legs moving, but it's still only a few hundred feet from my car to the grocery store entrance. While I might see a few friendly faces of people from my neighborhood while shopping, I am primarily focused on checking off items on my grocery list. After wheeling the bags of groceries out in my cart, I drive the five miles back to my house. My entire journey clocks in at a little under two hours, depending on traffic and how long my grocery list is.

When I run errands in Georgetown, it's a completely different story. I make plans to meet up with a friend for lunch at Sweetgreen, a salad shop on Wisconsin Avenue in Georgetown. The mile-long walk there from my house takes about 15 minutes. We sit outside for nearly an hour, talking and eating and people-watching. There's a cupcake shop one block over, so we stop in for a sweet treat. Parting ways with my friend, I walk about half a mile up Wisconsin Avenue to the CVS to pick up a prescription. On the way, I pass by Zara's window displays and enter the store to browse their selection, inevitably deciding to buy something. I resume my route to

CVS, now only three blocks away. After successfully picking up my prescription, I conclude my errands with a trip to Safeway, another half a mile up Wisconsin Avenue. Along the way, I run into a few friends who are headed in the opposite direction, and I stop briefly to chat. At the grocery store, I see even more familiar faces of fellow Georgetown students who frequent this particular location. I load up my reusable grocery bags and walk the remaining half of a mile home, one bag on each shoulder. I return to my house nearly four hours after my initial departure, having walked at least three miles.

While the three core tasks are the same — getting lunch, picking up a prescription, and going grocery shopping — the experiences are entirely different. I tend to spend a lot more money and time during my urban errands, but I also get more exercise and have a greater sense of enjoyment. When I'm at home, errands are a necessary, inconvenient part of my day. At school, however, the errands quickly turn into a full-day experience.

While hopping in and out of my car during my suburban errands is a nuisance, I cherish the chance to spend the day in the Georgetown neighborhood, and I can easily walk from one destination to another in roughly half-mile increments.

"At the end of the day, placemaking means that someone might do the same three things, but they will linger and have a cup of coffee, or browse in the boutique next door, or extend the stay, increase the spend, and decide it was so great they want to live there," Adam says.

Placemaking is a powerful tool for creating economic value. Still, there are obstacles to sharing that value in an equitable way.

WALKING THE HIGH LINE

"It's so much more than a walking trail," Adam says of New York City's High Line.

Located in the Chelsea borough, the High Line is a 1.4-mile-long elevated segment of New York Central Railroad's West Side Line that was transformed into a public park.

By definition, the High Line is just a walking trail. With well-cultivated plant life and expansive views of the Hudson River and the New York City skyline, the High Line is indeed an aesthetically pleasing place to walk. However, it has evolved to offer tours, stargazing opportunities, art showcases, camps for kids, and other seasonal events. Expert placemaking transformed the High Line into a destination all its own and a driver of economic growth in the surrounding neighborhood.

Constructed in the 1930s, the original rail line had fallen into disrepair and was scheduled for demolition. In the 1980s, Chelsea residents successfully blocked demolition in a court case. In 1999, the Friends of High Line was founded to advocate for preserving and repurposing the space for public use. After years of planning, the High Line first opened in 2009 and was completed in 2014.

When they initially made their case for the High Line's preservation, the Friends estimated that the park would attract 400,000 tourists and would boost New York City tax revenues by $250 million.

The $273 million project attracted five million tourists in 2014 alone. The High Line has boosted the city's tax revenues by $900 million and has spurred billions of dollars of economic development in the surrounding Chelsea area.

* * *

While the project's popularity has without a doubt benefitted the city, much of the High Line's extreme success has occurred at the expense of the Chelsea neighborhood's original inhabitants.

The High Line can be credited — at least in part — with augmenting the popularity of the surrounding neighborhood. Prior to the rebuilding project, the High Line was an abandoned railway and the Chelsea neighborhood did not attract a lot of visitors. Now, the throngs of tourists visiting the High Line frequent the neighborhood's restaurants and bars, the Chelsea Market, the Chelsea Piers recreational complex, and other local attractions. No article or feature about the High Line is complete without a list of restaurants and things to do nearby. The neighborhood's walkability encourages people to stay for longer periods of time and spend more money, and new businesses have flocked to the neighborhood because of its surge in popularity.

The story of the High Line's overwhelming success has spread around the world, but the story that receives much less press is how the project has negatively impacted the residents of the Chelsea neighborhood.

While nearly one-third of the Chelsea neighborhood residents are people of color, the overwhelming majority of High Line visitors are white. Not only do locals not benefit from the park itself but also they have not benefited from the economic windfall.

New condos are being constructed adjacent to the High Line with price tags as high as $6,000 per square foot, nearly three times the area's typical rate, according to real estate expert David Barista. Even the neighborhood's original gentrifiers are being priced out, leaving behind only the most expensive art galleries and Manhattan's elite. To further complicate matters, West Chelsea was rezoned in 2005 with minimal mandates for affordable housing, meaning that forces of gentrification will continue to push Chelsea's working-class residents out of the neighborhood.

"Once-thriving restaurants like La Lunchonette and Hector's diner, a local diner since 1949, have lost their customer base. Hardest hit have been the multigenerational businesses of 'gasoline alley.' Mostly auto-related establishments that don't fit into Michael R. Bloomberg's luxury city vision, several vanished in mere months, like species in a meteoric mass extinction. Bear Auto Shop was out after decades; the Olympia parking garage, after 35 years, closed when its rent reportedly quintupled," states Jeremiah Moss in a *New York Times* Opinion piece called "Disney World on the Hudson."

While name brand additions to the neighborhood have thrived, small businesses have suffered as a result of the neighborhood's changing dynamic. The throngs of tourists visiting the neighborhood are looking for trendy new restaurants rather than neighborhood mainstays. In the face of the gentrification brought on by the adjusted zoning laws and booming tourism, the High Line has emerged as a local symbol of Manhattan's increasing inequality.

"We were from the community. We wanted to do it for the

neighborhood. Ultimately, we failed," High Line co-founder Robert Hammond said in an interview with *CityLab*.

Hammond and his co-founder Joshua David are trying to remedy some of the damage. Part of their initiative has been to convene designers and planners to determine strategies for promoting the inclusivity of public parks. While the co-founders did convene local residents in designing the High Line, they primarily discussed physical characteristics as opposed to how the park would respond to the local community's needs.

"Instead of asking what the design should look like, I wish we'd asked, 'What can we do for you?'" Hammond reflects in the *CityLab* interview. "Because people have bigger problems than design."

As the founders learned, it's essential for public places to be the product of public discussion, which should occur early and often in the planning process. In 2011, two years after the High Line's initial construction, the co-founders met with local residents to discuss their specific needs, this time focusing on issues beyond design.

"What people really needed were jobs and a more affordable cost of living," they discovered. Hammond says that they also found that residents stayed away from the High Line for three primary reasons: "They didn't feel it was built for them; they didn't see people who looked like them using it; and they didn't like the park's mulch-heavy programming."

In response, Friends of the High Line implemented job-training programs for teenagers as well as cultural events within the public housing campuses, away from the swarms of tourists. In the face of the High Line's explosive growth, it may be too little too late to reverse the job loss and gentrification.

The High Line team members are determined to share their knowledge with future public space initiatives. While they never could have predicted the extent to which the High Line would contribute to the changing fabric of the Chelsea neighborhood, they are committed to ensuring that future projects do not repeat their mistakes.

The key to effective public spaces, the High Line planners now recognize, is engaging community members throughout the planning process in order to anticipate and brainstorm solutions for community members' concerns. The High Line could have collaborated with the local community to advocate for affordable housing in the neighborhood or to set up a way for community members to share in the project's economic windfall.

The High Line team is working with Atlanta's BeltLine, a project that's notably focused on promoting equity through public spaces. Although planners were conscious of the BeltLine's potential for gentrification, the project's rapid development triggered sharp increases in home values. The BeltLine team had to work quickly to revise the city's zoning laws in order to maintain affordability in neighborhoods with increasing demand.

"The problems are essentially financial, and there are ways to fix them, whether it's traditional tax credits, subsidies to renters, inclusive zoning, land value capture, or clearing paths in zoning codes for snug accommodations like accessory dwelling units or tiny homes," *CityLab* argues. "Not every tool is right for every city. But tools do exist."

Walkability is a powerful agent of placemaking and economic prosperity. In order to realize the full economic potential of walkability, it is essential that government decision-makers and private developers work with local communities to ensure that walkable spaces serve community needs in an inclusive way.

Policy change and walkable design are two good places to start in order to enhance the positive economic impact of walkability.

EQUAL OPPORTUNITY + WALKABLE DESIGN

"It wasn't that many years ago that walkable urban places had a price *penalty* associated with them, not a price premium," says Christopher Leinberger.

In 2012, Christopher and his colleague Mariela Alfonzo, researchers at the Brookings Institution think tank in Washington, D.C., published a groundbreaking report, "Walk this Way: The Economic Promise of Walkable Places in Metropolitan Washington, D.C." They found a direct correlation between walkability and economic performance, quantifying a belief that urbanists often take for granted.

This connection between walkable places and economic promise hasn't always been the case. Only a few decades ago, some of today's most walkable and desirable neighborhoods were inner-city neighborhoods. Abandoned by the middle class during urban sprawl, these neighborhoods were a source of inexpensive housing. Now, housing prices in walkable neighborhoods are exploding while gentrification forces less affluent people into less walkable neighborhoods.

"[There's been a] structural shift," Leinberger asserts. "And when you have a structural shift, it's important to change your public policy to take it into consideration."

When implemented strategically, walkability is capable of

bridging economic divides. With the current supply-demand mismatch driving up prices in walkable places, Leinberger and Alfonzo recommend that both the private and public sectors invest in and promote walkability.

Along with policy, thoughtful urban design can be a tool for equal economic opportunity, as I learned from a conversation with Demetrio Scopelliti, the Advisor to the Deputy Mayor of Milan, Italy, for Urban Planning. Despite the six-hour time difference between D.C. and Milan, we found time to talk on the phone about Demetrio's experience as an urban designer.

"How do you incorporate walkability without suffering the negative consequences of gentrification?" I asked Demetrio, with the example of the High Line at the forefront of my mind.

"Distribute the impact by creating small walkable centers throughout the city instead of just one," Demetrio recommended. "Gentrification isn't always bad if it is planned and controlled."

Having just one walkable boulevard will bring all of the people to that one location and will amplify the negative effects of gentrification, Demetrio explained. Despite the good intentions of walkability, some successful pedestrian streets become too touristy and impersonal when they become too much of an attraction. Having many different walkable spaces distributes the economic benefits more evenly, creating small centers throughout the city instead of just one. Demetrio is working to implement this kind of walkability in Milan.

"The pace at which Milan intends to turn its city core car-free is slower than most," reads a *CityLab* article on the city's plan to pedestrianize.

The slow pace at which Milan is transforming its streets to pedestrian-only is deliberate. By gradually implementing walkability on a street-by-street basis, the city is hoping to slowly increase the appeal and economic prosperity of the parts of the city that are becoming walkable, in order to avoid the negative effects of rapid gentrification. The slow pace of change also allows Milan's residents to offer input into the process and to gradually adjust their lifestyles to become less dependent on car transportation in the city.

Demetrio's work shows that thoughtful planning is a critical tool in promoting equal economic opportunity through walkable urban design. Still, making walkability work is contingent on other transportation modes.

It sounds counterintuitive. Isn't the whole point of walkability to promote walking over other modes of transportation?

According to Devon McAslan, a Ph.D. candidate in urban

planning at the University of Michigan, walkability is about effectively incorporating walking in with other modes of transportation. Simply put, you can't have walkability without other forms of transportation.

As is the case in many cities around the world, all modes of transportation are expected to share the road. Having cars, buses, bikes, and pedestrians all share the same streets leads to a less-than-ideal situation for all parties involved. Think: traffic, accidents, road rage, etc.

Devon's research on the theory of urban fabrics focuses on how these different transportation modes can better coexist. In the field of urban planning, the theory of urban fabrics recognizes that cities are combinations of three different transportation modes: pedestrians, public transit, and automobiles. Instead of designing cities for all three kinds of transportation to coexist, strategic urban planning can prioritize each type of transit in the fabric where it dominates. An ideal city according to the theory would have cars driving into the city and public transit managing transportation between the city's neighborhoods, with pedestrians dominating the streets within each neighborhood.

This model is a strong departure from the majority of cities that prioritize automobiles at the expense of pedestrians. Devon believes that walkability — and equal access to walkability

— can be enhanced through strategic relationships with other forms of transportation, especially public transit.

The problem with public transit in the way the system currently operates is that it connects automobile transportation at one end to walking at the other, without connecting walkable neighborhoods to each other. In a world where not all neighborhoods have equal access to walkability and walkable neighborhoods often exist in isolation, walkability is limited in nature and the benefits of walkable neighborhoods are not accessible to everyone.

Public transportation has the potential to make walkability accessible to a greater number of people — not just the people who can afford to live in the most walkable neighborhoods. Going hand-in-hand with Demetrio's recommendation to have multiple walkable urban centers, Devon recommends connecting walkable neighborhoods with each other via public transit. This public investment can share the benefits of walking as well as boost the economic performance of each walkable neighborhood.

Although it seems counterintuitive, improving public transportation benefits walking behavior in cities. According to Devon's research, people who use public transit actually walk more than those who do not. They are also willing to walk further to use their transit. With better public transportation between walking centers and from walking centers to automobiles, you can incorporate walking throughout your transportation instead of sitting in a car for your entire journey. Well-planned transportation systems allow you to take part in the best aspects of each form of transportation — particularly, the innumerable benefits of incorporating walking into your day.

Walkability can't exist in isolation. The whole transportation system has to work together to facilitate walking when it makes sense and other forms of transportation when walking isn't feasible.

While redesigning transportation systems is not work that can be done overnight, it is promising to envision a future where transportation systems are designed with walkability at their core. Imagine less time wasted in traffic, healthier individuals, more vibrant places, livelier streets...

The bottom line is that urban planning has an important influence on walkability and economic performance. It can influence the speed at which a neighborhood is gentrified, the kind of encounters that take place in a space, and the overall desirability of a neighborhood. Together, policymakers, planners, businesspeople, and other stakeholders have a responsibility to plan walkability and transportation in a way that promotes equal economic opportunity.

Not long ago, cars were the engine driving economic growth. Now, all signs point to walking as the path forward, as walkable urban areas gain popularity over drivable suburban ones. As demonstrated by the examples of New York City's High Line and Atlanta's BeltLine, taking advantage of the full potential of the walking economy will require the collaborative participation of all of the people who shape the development process, from planners and private developers to public sector actors and citizens, in order to prioritize pedestrians in all planning decisions.

STEP 9.

NEXT STEPS

———

Obesity. A mental health crisis. Conflict. Injustice. Cancer. Climate change. Inequality.

There's a lot of problems to be solved. Throughout the preceding eight steps, we've discovered that walking is a first step in solving these problems and more. These changes begin with the individual, are amplified by groups, and challenge the status quo of societies.

Still, there are some greater societal shifts that must occur in order to create the kind of lasting change that will truly make the world a better place.

What the best way to kickstart the creative problem-solving required to change the world for the better?

As you may have guessed, the answer is none other than... walking.

THE SECRET TO GREATER PRODUCTIVITY

Ted Eytan isn't a normal doctor, a fact he made clear from our very first exchange. Upon addressing him as "Dr. Eytan," he swiftly replied, "Please call me Ted, I don't use the 'D' word."

His full name is an alphabet soup of post-nominal letters: "Ted Eytan, MD, MS, MPH." With a Doctor of Medicine from the University of Arizona College of Medicine, a Master of Public Health from the University of California, Berkley, and a Master of Science in Health Services from the University of Washington, it goes without saying that Ted is an expert in his field of public health.

When he entered the working world after his many years as a student, Ted found himself sitting much more frequently than he would have liked. Whether it was attending meetings in a conference room or doing work at his desk all day, Ted slowly recognized the negative impacts of his new sedentary lifestyle. He felt less healthy and more sluggish. His ability to think creatively was stifled.

Ted began to notice that many of his most creative ideas in school had come about when he was moving around during the day. His years of schooling had provided him with the opportunity to walk around campus and catch up with fellow classmates throughout the day. Through these interactions with peers and the outside world, he was able to fully engage with his surrounding environment at critical moments every day. While at work, he missed these daily moments of walking.

Then, something turned his working life around: a walking contest.

While Ted was working at the Group Health Cooperative in the early 2000s, his office decided to have a walking contest in which each person tracked their daily steps on a pedometer. Even though it was a small change, it shifted the culture of his office from being sedentary to being active.

"This is what work is supposed to be," he thought.

Experiencing enhanced physical activity during the workday boosted Ted's creative thinking. He had the chance to connect with the community in and around his office, and he had a better sense of what was happening in the world around him. All of this resulted from the simple introduction of more steps into his workday.

From then on, Ted has strongly advocated for active lifestyles in the workplace, particularly through walking meetings.

According to Ted, traditional modes of education indicate that the best way to learn is by sitting and "looking at someone for hours on end." Ted believes that this actually stifles creativity. Movement, as Ted has learned as a doctor, is a more effective way of learning. For the same reasons that he refuses to use the "D" word, Ted believes that in order to effectively teach, a teacher must learn about the people he or she is teaching. In order to effectively meet with someone, you must learn about the person you are meeting with.

And what better way to do that than by moving together?

When you exercise, your brain actually regenerates, as you learned in Step 3. Exercise is scientifically proven to change the way your brain operates, helping you better manage your environment and respond to stress more effectively. Learning and moving go hand-in-hand.

Walking together also stimulates interpersonal connection and trust, according to Lawrence Williams and John Bargh's research on interpersonal warmth.

Instead of inducing sleep or enabling distraction — as many meetings do — walking meetings encourage creativity, connection, and mental performance. Given the strong evidence in favor of walking meetings, Ted wanted to share his passion for walking meetings with others.

★ ★ ★

"How can I convince people of the power of walking meetings?" he thought.

Ted was scheduled to present at the Every Body Walk! 2013 Walking Summit in Washington, D.C. It turned out to the perfect opportunity to share — and test — his message.

When it came time for Ted to present, he could see that many of the people sitting in the audience looked bored or on the verge of falling asleep.

"They have no idea what they're in for," he thought as he stood in front of the Walking Summit participants, ready to begin his presentation.

"Who's never gone on a walking meeting in their life?" he asked the crowd. Ted was surprised that there were people — at a Walking Summit, no less — who had never experienced a walking meeting before.

After highlighting the benefits of walking and walking meetings, Ted continued. "We've been taught that a meeting starts when you arrive somewhere and sit down. A meeting doesn't have to start when you sit down. Actually, we're all going on a walking meeting and it starts right now."

He could hear murmurs of confusion from the crowd. After the initial surprise set in, the bored and sleeping participants started to sit up taller in their chairs, looking ready to move.

"I want everyone to tweet that they went on a walking meeting," Ted instructed, "so we can change people's models about what a meeting is."

Improving walkability and encouraging more effective meetings in the future depends on changing the culture surrounding meetings, according to Ted. We must change the definition of a meeting from the narrow context of people sitting across from each other at a desk or in a conference room. Social media, Ted believes, is a great tool for creating norms around walking meetings.

"All right, let's do it!" he announced to the crowd.

And, just like that, the 1,000 Summit participants got out of their chairs, storming the conference center's elevators and stairwells to head outside for their walking meeting in the surrounding D.C. neighborhood.

Prior to the Walking Summit, Ted wanted to debunk the commonly held belief that it's impossible to have a walking meeting with more than two people. He demonstrated that it was indeed possible — with 1,000 test subjects.

Upon returning from the walking meeting, attendees who had previously not spoken to each other were smiling and laughing, and he could sense a renewed energy among the Summit attendees. Although the walking meeting lasted only 15 minutes, the change in the spirit of the attendees during that short amount of time was transformative.

* * *

Ted's promotion of walking meetings is qualified by some clear ground rules to ensure inclusivity and effectiveness. According to Ted, it's imperative never to surprise someone with a walking meeting. A meeting of this nature often requires preparation in the form of proper clothing and footwear, and the somewhat foreign concept of a walking meeting may be a source of discomfort if it's sprung on someone at the last minute. It's also important to acknowledge that people are mobile in different ways and to make accommodations accordingly.

Prior to moving to Washington, D.C., Ted lived in Seattle, Washington, where the hilly terrain can prove prohibitive to someone who isn't comfortable walking up an incline. One time, he proposed a walking meeting to a colleague, who responded that she was not physically able to walk up hills. In order to accommodate her needs and also her desire to take part in a walking meeting, Ted offered to walk downhill together and then share a taxi for the return route up the hill. Taking steps to account for accessibility and inclusion are essential factors of a successful walking meeting.

As Ted has learned through his walking meeting experiences, when meetings are moved out of the narrow confines of a traditional office space, a meeting of two or more people becomes an opportunity for developing trust and confidence, enhancing creativity, promoting health, and optimizing mental performance. A cultural shift towards walking has the power to redefine societal norms around productivity and creativity.

A CREATIVITY BOOST

"There is something truly compelling about blockchain technology's potential beyond Bitcoin," Lara Fishbane asserted in a Beeck Center for Social Impact + Innovation publication. "We want to ensure that decision makers in the blockchain space have a toolset for driving social good with this promising technology while reducing harm to the user."

You don't have to understand the inner workings of blockchain to know that Lara's work is having an impact. An expert on the ethics of emerging technology such as blockchain, Lara is helping imagine ways in which new technology can be applied for good. Lara graduated from Georgetown University in 2017 with a double major in English and Economics and a passion for changing the world. Wise beyond her years, Lara is already asserting herself as a leading voice of the social sector by attending conferences, writing blog posts, and convening communities around her research areas of public policy and data and technology for social good.

I first met Lara while working as a student analyst at the Beeck Center, a think tank and social innovation hub on Georgetown's campus. In my short time of knowing Lara, she has become one of my greatest role models due to her determination to see the good in the world and in other people.

On one unseasonably warm day in February after work, I had the chance to talk candidly to Lara about her experience transitioning into the working world. Although she had previously held a number of internships, including an editorial internship at Forbes, Lara was caught off-guard by just how challenging it was to adjust to working full-time after graduating from college.

"Sitting in a room for nine hours and not moving will make you go insane," she told me.

As someone preparing to make my own transition into the working world, this was not exactly what I was hoping to hear.

Whereas her college schedule required her to move consistently throughout the day from her dorm to class to student activity meetings and more, Lara found her work lifestyle to be much more sedentary. During the workday, Lara would sit in the Beeck Center's open office workspace for hours at a time. With almost everything she needed during the workday located in the office, few things necessitated leaving the confines of the Beeck Center space.

"You interact with so few things that are real," Lara reflected. "You're just staring into a screen and are surrounded by walls and by other people who are all on screens."

While technology can be an enabler of creativity, it cannot be the method of attaining creativity all of the time.

* * *

Sitting in front of a screen is simply not the optimal scenario for generating your most creative ideas. Marily Oppezzo, a researcher at Stanford University, provides an alternative for creative idea generation in her aptly-named TED Talk: "Want to be more creative? Go for a walk."

"The creative process from the first idea to the final product, is a long process. It's super-iterative, lots of refinement, blood, sweat, tears, and years. We're not saying you're going to go out for a walk and come back with the Sistine Chapel in your left hand," Marily says in the talk, qualifying her claim that walking enhances creativity for a skeptical crowd.

Still, Marily's research clearly demonstrates that walking improves one's ability to think creatively. In her study, test subjects had four minutes to brainstorm as many alternate uses for everyday objects as possible, such as uses for a key other than opening a lock. The standard for whether an idea was creative was "appropriate novelty," meaning that the idea had to be realistic and could not have been said by anyone else in the population surveyed.

Here's one idea from the study that was deemed to be a creative use for a key: "If you were dying and it was a murder mystery, and you had to carve the name of the murderer into the ground with your dying words."

Indeed, it fits the criteria of being both appropriate and novel.

Two rounds of tests were performed on three different groups of subjects who were either seated or walking on a treadmill. One group sat for both tests, while another group sat first and then walked, and the final group walked and then sat. Both of the groups that sat for the first test generated a similar average number of creative ideas, whereas the group that walked on a treadmill had almost twice as many creative ideas.

For the second test, the group that sat twice didn't show any improvement from the first test. However, the people in the group that sat for the first test and walked for the second one almost doubled their creativity.

To Marily, the most interesting result was in the group that walked for the first test and then sat: "The people who were walking on the treadmill still had a residue effect of the walking, and they were still creative afterwards." Even though their creativity did decline when they sat, those who walked and then sat were significantly more creative than the people in the groups that sat for the first test.

Despite the fact that the treadmill was located in a windowless room — seemingly an environment that would stifle creativity — the differences in performance between the sitters and the walkers are truly astonishing. In order to take advantage of the creativity-enhancing benefits of walking, Marily has five suggestions:

1. Pick a defined problem to brainstorm during your walk ahead of time. This will add structure to your brainstorming session.
2. Walk at a pace that is comfortable for you. "If I were running, the only idea I would have would be to stop running," Marily jokes.
3. Don't lock in on your first idea. Keep coming up with new ideas.
4. Speak and record your new ideas using a smartphone or other

recording device. The act of writing down your ideas can be a filter to creativity.

5. Don't force yourself to keep walking if the creative ideas are not coming. You can always take a break and start walking again later.

Marily's steps for walking to enhance creativity are practical and easy to implement. Still, a cultural shift is required to make walking for creative problem-solving a reality.

* * *

In the working world, Lara feels that it is frowned upon to decide to get up and go for a walk, especially if it's not associated with a productive task as in the case of a walking meeting or an errand.

The American economy values people's time on an hourly basis. There's a pressure to constantly become more productive and more efficient. Any kind of break — especially getting up to go for a walk — is often held in a negative light.

"Walking offers an escape from the workday," Lara told me. She's found that walking provides her with an opportunity to quite literally step away from her work and to clear her head. When she returns to her desk, she can work more efficiently and effectively. Contrary to popular belief, breaks actually increase productivity.

"Sitting can kill you," Lara added, reminding me of just how damaging the culture of sitting at a desk all day can be. Sitting for long periods of time — no matter how much you exercise — is a risk factor for early death. With this knowledge, Lara believes that it is essential to concertedly insert opportunities to walk into her daily routine, such as walking the last mile from the Metro to work instead of taking the bus whenever possible. Otherwise, she would spend most of her life sleeping, sitting on the Metro, and sitting all day at work.

As an avid hiker, climber, and explorer of nature, Lara believes that walking provides her with an important reminder during the workday of the world that exists beyond the confines of her office space. On weekends, Lara enjoys hiking on trails in and around D.C., which she believes offers her a chance to step away from the work week in a more revitalizing way than leaving her desk behind for a few minutes to take a walking break.

"Walking reminds me that my screen isn't the most important thing," Lara said.

Walking allows her to put her work into perspective and to think about how her work fits into the larger landscape of the world. Moving through the world as it exists in the present permits Lara to envision how it could be in the future.

Lara, a leading voice on the intersection between social impact and emerging technology, has found that her work is enhanced by the simple act of taking a break to go for a walk. In order to inspire creative thought, minimize burnout, and maximize the impact of leading change-makers such as Lara, walking and other forms of productive breaks must be prioritized in the workplace. Changing norms around walking breaks can be as simple as asking someone to go for a walk or tweeting about the act of taking a walking meeting.

When it comes to making walking the rule rather than the exception, individuals have a responsibility to use these techniques to create a culture shift around what it means to be productive. This shift is already being embraced by some of the world's most influential people.

THE MOST POWERFUL PEOPLE ARE PEDESTRIANS

From history's greatest minds to the people shaping the technological revolution today, society's leading change-makers have already discovered that walking is the key to solving all kinds of problems. If you're not already convinced of the power of pedestrians in changing the world, maybe some of these people will change your mind...

Albert Einstein, the father of modern physics, was without a doubt one of the most influential people of the 20th century. Throughout his life, Einstein was known — of course, secondarily to his influence on the field of science — for his love of daily walks. While working on Unified Field Theory in the U.S., Einstein walked 1.5 miles each way between his home and Princeton University. Although he certainly recognized the physical fitness and memory-boosting benefits of walking, he also walked for purposes of creativity and problem-solving. When it came to working out problems in his head, he found it most useful to go for a walk.

Henry David Thoreau, a 19th-century naturalist and philosopher, is today considered one of the United States' most influential authors as well as the intellectual foundation of the environmental conservation movement. In "Walking," one of his most famous essays published in *The Atlantic*, Thoreau reflects on his own relationship with walking: "I think that I cannot preserve my health and spirits, unless I spend four hours a day at least — and it is commonly more than that — sauntering through the woods and over the hills and fields, absolutely free from all worldly engagements." While having that much daily time to spend alone in nature is a luxury for most, Thoreau recognized the essential point that the best way to understand nature and to let one's mind wander is through walking. Thoreau wasn't a proponent of walking for a specific purpose such as exercise. Instead, he believed that walking should be "itself the enterprise and adventure of the day," a practice that he refers to as the art of sauntering.

Michelle and Barack Obama, one of the world's most powerful couples, are leading the charge on walking in the 21st century. As the 44th President of the United States, Barack Obama preferred to "walk and talk" to increase the productivity of his meetings. On one occasion, he went on a walking tour of Krün, Germany, with German Chancellor Angela Merkel, and they greeted locals together. At home in the United States, the President was known to leave the White House property to walk the streets of the nation's capital and talk to the people he encountered.

As the First Lady of the United States, Michelle Obama prioritized children's health and activity through her *Let's Move!* campaign. According to the First Lady, one of the easiest ways to get kids moving is by walking. She endorsed walking school buses as a way for kids, led by adult chaperones, to get exercise on the way to school. The First Lady and *Let's Move!* participated in Fitbit's Step It Up! challenge, in which 615,390 people walked almost 61 billion steps over the course of two weeks. Michelle Obama has used her public voice to amplify the importance of physical activity in daily life.

Steve Jobs, CEO of Apple from 1997 to 2011, changed the way the world works, from making technology simpler and more accessible to transforming the way that business is run. His ability to ruthlessly tweak and refine products and processes forever altered the technology industry, and his habit of walking barefoot is symbolic of his refusal to play by the rules. Throughout his life, Steve relied on walking for fitness, mindfulness, problem-solving, and creativity. "If there was something that Steve wanted to talk about, and there always was, we'd go for a walk," said Jobs' best friend, Oracle Chairman and CTO Larry Ellison. It was while on a hike with Ellison that Steve brainstormed his strategy for regaining control of Apple after being fired in 1985. When it came to meeting new people, especially potential new hires, Steve preferred to meet while walking because conversation flowed more naturally and there weren't as many distractions as in a bustling workplace.

Following in the footsteps of Steve Jobs, Facebook CEO Mark Zuckerberg is another impactful proponent of walking meetings. He's forever changed what it means to communicate, and his social network has had an "enormous impact in diverse realms — including politics, media, marketing, privacy, our sense of identity and our definition of friendship." Many of Facebook's strategic decisions were made during walking meetings. After a series of hour-long walks around Silicon Valley with WhatsApp founder Jan Koum, Mark successfully sealed the deal for Facebook to acquire WhatsApp for $19 billion. In another walking meeting with Facebook Graph Search lead engineer Lars Rasmussen, Mark had seemingly perfectly planned the timing of his speech and the trail, so that the pair reached the top of a mountain and an expansive view of the Valley as Mark concluded his talk.

On a few occasions, Steve Jobs and Mark Zuckerberg were spotted walking together in Palo Alto discussing a potential partnership wherein Apple's music social network service, Ping, would be incorporated into Facebook. Although the deal never went through, one can only imagine what two of the tech industry's most powerful people said during their time walking together.

Jobs' and Zuckerberg's habit of taking walking meetings has now taken the technology industry by storm. Nilofer Merchant's 2013 TED Talk, "Got a meeting? Take a walk" can be held at least partially responsible.

Nilofer, a Silicon Valley-based author, speaker, and business-woman, was admittedly skeptical when a colleague first asked her if they could conduct their meeting while walking because he needed to walk his dog. Now, she logs 20 to 30 miles of walking meetings per week and has become one of walking's greatest proponents.

"Sitting has become the smoking of our generation," Nilofer asserts in her TED Talk.

Everyone is sitting all of the time, so no one questions how bad the habit is for your health. And even if you do know how bad sitting is for you, it's a difficult practice to change because of how commonplace it is. While Nilofer used to think that you either had to take care of your health or your obligations, she's found that walking meetings allow you to achieve both at the same time. Walking, she believes, actually makes her meetings more efficient and effective.

"There's this amazing thing about getting out of the box that leads to out-of-the-box thinking," Nilofer says in her talk, encouraging everyone to try a walking meeting.

Greg Gottesman, a startup founder and venture capitalist, is another tech guru who advocates for walking in the workplace.

"We as human beings, when we're forced to sit and stare at one another, it's harder to be open and creative and it just makes for a more stilted interaction, especially if you don't know someone well," Greg has observed. "When you have a walking meeting and you don't have to sit and stare at someone, it tends to feel a little more informal, people tend to be more open and creative, you can cover a wider range of topics, and people are more honest."

He's witnessed firsthand — whether it's during discussions with his wife or in meetings with colleagues — that walking opens up the potential for participants to bring their best selves to the table. In the context of a more accessible environment, Greg believes that walking meeting participants get to know each other better in both the business and personal realms. This is when people's best, most creative ideas are brought to life.

I could fill an entire book with the stories of influential people who go for walks. But the bottom line is that many of the world's most prominent change-makers already recognize the power of walking in improving creativity and enhancing problem-solving capabilities. Not only are some of the world's most powerful people pedestrians, but also simply being a pedestrian gives you access to world-changing power.

ENVISIONING CHANGE

Changing the world requires the ability to see the world differently and to recognize its potential.

As the Advisor to the Deputy Mayor for Urban Planning, Green Areas, and Agriculture of Milan, Italy, Demetrio Scopelliti has a clear vision of a walkable, car-free future for the city. Milan has already adopted a section of walkable streets in the city center, and the Deputy Mayor has plans to transition the city towards a walkable future.

"I am fascinated by how architecture and urban design affect people's behaviours and social life, particularly in streets and public spaces," Demetrio states in his LinkedIn profile. Intuitively, this connection between urban design and social behavior makes sense. In a city, streets are the stage on which people live their lives, so cities should be designed in a way that permits people to thrive. But this isn't always the case.

According to Demetrio, most city planners know everything about cars and how they move in a space and how to design roads for them. When it comes to pedestrians, however, planners have an incomplete understanding of how they use a space.

"If you plan cities for cars and traffic, you get cars and traffic. If you plan for people and places, you get people and places," says Fred Kent, the founder of the Project for Public Spaces.

In his role as an urban designer, Demetrio cares deeply about how people move in a space. And the only way that Demetrio feels he can design a place that works for the people who use it is by walking in it. Being physically present in the space that he is designing — with the people for whom he is designing it — allows Demetrio to boost his creativity and to solve the problems facing the people who interact with the space.

"I cannot understand a place, and I cannot imagine the space if

I don't walk through it," Demetrio states simply. For Demetrio, walking is a tool for discovery, understanding, observation, inspiration, and much more.

Demetrio cherishes the experience of walking in a public space — from exchanging a friendly smile with a stranger to knowing that he is minimizing his environmental footprint — and he wants to design spaces that give all people access to those kinds of experiences.

"There is no successful city where there is no life in the streets," he asserts, recognizing that thoughtful design has positive implications for all of society.

Demetrio's vision is already coming to fruition. The process of Milan's pedestrianization is a slow and collaborative one, with input from citizens and competitions for public design solutions at the core of the city's new urban strategy. In one experimental project called #nevicata14 ("snowfall of 2014"), Piazza Castello, the city's second largest square, was temporarily made pedestrian-only. Free Wi-Fi, smart lighting, and public seating, as well as special events, performances, and classes transformed the square into a place that was appealing to pedestrians, increasing foot traffic and allowing citizens to congregate to collaborate on more projects with the common good in mind.

Not only does walking open up the potential for better design, but also better-designed spaces facilitate the ability to walk for a better world.

This book is full of the stories of people who, like Demetrio, had a clear vision of the kind of world that they wanted to create. Jim Walker wanted to make the world a more walkable place. Ted Eytan saw the potential for healthier individuals. Sarah Stiles envisioned a future of mental wellness. Osnat Ita Skoblinski dreamed of peace between sworn enemies. Mahatma Gandhi worked towards independence. Greer Richey fundraised for a world without cancer. John Francis believed in a sustainable future. Adam Ducker saw the potential for thriving local economies.

Each of these change-makers recognized their individual power in shaping the world. And, each of these change-makers embraced walking as a vehicle of change, enacting their vision of the world by starting with a single step.

———

Walking is something we do every day. It's the way to get from one place to another. It's a necessary, at times inconvenient, part of life.

And it's one of the most accessible tools for changing the world.

Feeling out of shape, mentally worn out, or like what you do doesn't matter? Go for a walk.

Trying to better understand your world, stand up for something you believe in, or promote a cause that's important to you? Go for a walk.

Wanting to combat climate change, boost the economy, or find inspiration? Go for a walk.

If you're already walking, challenge yourself to walk more and encourage others to do the same. Think of new ways that you can channel your steps into impact.

If you don't like walking, find a walking buddy. A companion can turn dreaded physical exertion into a fun adventure.

If you don't have time to walk, make time. After all, sitting takes years off of your life. A few minutes of walking now will pay dividends later.

And if you don't know where to start, just start. The beauty of walking is that you never know where your feet might take you.

I've said it before, and I'll say it again: Pedestrians have a lot of power. A person will take an average of 216,262,500 steps in their lifetime. That's the equivalent of walking five times around the equator.

With every single step, you transform a place just by being present in it. What kind of mark do you want your steps to leave?

While this book offers ideas for channeling your steps into impact, it's up to you to determine what kind of an impact you want your steps to make.

So, what are you waiting for?

The journey towards a better world starts with a single step.

NOTES

EXPERT INTERVIEWS:

Dr. Sarah Stiles, Professor of Sociology, Georgetown University, 15 Mar. 2018

Dr. Ted Eytan, Medical Director, Kaiser Permanente Center for Total Health, 13 Feb. 2018

Jim Walker, Strategic Director and Founder, Walk21, 23 Feb. 2018.

Katherine "Kate" Kraft, Executive Director, America Walks, 20 Feb. 2018.

Thomas "Tom" Richards, Director of Community Engagement, American Council on Exercise, 19 Feb. 2018.

Eugénie "Nina" Lund-Simon, Psychology Major, Georgetown University College Class of 2018, 11 Feb. 2018.

Dr. Jenny Roe, Director of the Center for Design + Health,

University of Virginia School of Architecture, 23 Mar. 2018.

Adam Ducker, Director of Urban Real Estate, Robert Charles Lesser & Co. (RCLCO), 16 Feb. 2018.

Dr. John Francis, Planetwalker, Author of *Planetwalker: How to Change Your World One Step at a Time*, 25 Feb. 2018.

Jason Nellis, Head of Marketing, Packagd, 1 Mar. 2018.

Dr. Ellen Badone, Professor of Anthropology, McMaster University, 2 Mar. 2018.

Breanne Butler, Director of Capacity Building + Board Member, Women's March, 1 Mar. 2018.

Greer Richey, English Major, Georgetown University College Class of 2018, 11 Feb. 2018.

Emilie Cecil, Critical Care Registered Nurse, Johns Hopkins Hospital, 13 Mar. 2018.

Lara Fishbane, Research Assistant, The Brookings Institution, 15 Feb. 2018.

Demetrio Scopelliti, Advisor to the Deputy Mayor for Urban Planning, Green Areas and Agriculture, City of Milan, Italy, 23 Feb. 2018.

Dr. Devon McAslan, Doctor of Philosophy, Urban and Regional Planning, University of Michigan, 16 Feb. 2018.

Greg Gottesman, Managing Director and Co-Founder, Pioneer Square Labs, 1 Mar. 2018.

INTRODUCTION. SO, YOU WANT TO CHANGE THE WORLD?

More than a billion individuals: Mascarenhas, Hyacinth. "45

Surprising Facts About Extreme Poverty Around the World You May Not Have Realized." *Mic,* 22 May 2014, https://mic.com/articles/89717/45-surprising-facts-about-extreme-poverty-around-the-world-you-may-not-have-realized#.dtUaJzOeA.

STEP 1. PLACEMAKING

A person will take: SnowBrains. "Brain Post: How Far Does the Average Human Walk in a Lifetime?" *SnowBrains,* 20 June 2018, https://snowbrains.com/brain-post-how-far-does-the-average-human-walk-in-a-lifetime/.

WHO GETS TO WALK?

Dictionary.com defines walking: "Walking." *Dictionary.com,* 2018, www.dictionary.com/browse/walking?s=t.
My preferred definition: "Walk." *Merriam-Webster,* 2018, https://www.merriam-webster.com/dictionary/walk.

THE POWER OF PLACEMAKING

In one of the commute photos: Eytan, Ted. "2018.01.11 DC People and Places via #ActiveTransportation, Washington, DC USA." *Flickr,* Yahoo!, 12 Aug. 2018, www.flickr.com/photos/taedc/sets/72157691343788404/with/39630417421/.
In another photo: Eytan, Ted. "2018.01.11 DC People and Places via #ActiveTransportation, Washington, DC USA." *Flickr,* Yahoo!, 12 Aug. 2018, www.flickr.com/photos/taedc/

sets/72157691343788404/with/39630417421/.

"Strengthening the connection": "What is Placemaking? *Project for Public Spaces,* 2018, www.pps.org/article/what-is-placemaking.

TOWARDS A MORE WALKABLE WORLD

"Walkability is a word": "Dan Burden." *Project for Public Spaces,* 31 Dec. 2008, https://www.pps.org/article/dburden.

"Walking is an unspectacular natural": Adler, Michael. "Pedestrians are Anarchists." *Tipping Points,* 2018, tipping-points_Pedestrians_are_anarchists_interview.pdf.

Walk21's 16th conference: "Walk21-XVI: Vienna, Austria." *Walk21,* 2018, https://www.walk21.com/vienna.

Vienna's strategy around walkability: "Stepping Ahead: Walk21 Vienna 2015 Conference Magazine." *Walk21 Vienna,* 2015, https://www.wien.gv.at/stadtentwicklung/studien/pdf/b008449.pdf.

"As a fish needs to swim": Peñalosa, Enrique. "Why Buses Represent Democracy in Action." *TED: Ideas Worth Spreading,* 2018, https://www.ted.com/talks/enrique_penalosa_why_buses_represent_democracy_in_action/up-next.

COMPLETE STREETS

"At America Walks": "America Walks." *Commit to Inclusion,* 2018, http://committoinclusion.org/america-walks/.

"People who walk in low-income neighborhoods":

"Pedestrians Dying at Disproportionate Rates in America's Poorer Neighborhoods." *Governing,* 2018, http://www.governing.com/topics/public-justice-safety/gov-pedestrian-deaths-analysis.html.

African-American pedestrians: Seskin, Stephanie. "Dangerous by Design 2014 Highlights Preventable Pedestrian Fatalities." *Smart Growth America,* 20 May 2014, https://smartgrowthamerica.org/dangerous-by-design-2014-highlights-preventable-pedestrian-fatalities/.

"The places where we live": "Take Action." *America Walks,* 2018, http://americawalks.org/take-action/.

Every planning and infrastructure decision: "A People-Centered Transportation System." *Strong Towns Podcast,* Shout Engine, 27 Oct. 2016, http://shoutengine.com/StrongTownsPodcast/a-people-centered-transportation-system-25499.

"A Complete Streets approach": "National Complete Streets Coalition." *Smart Growth America,* 2018, https://smartgrowthamerica.org/program/national-complete-streets-coalition/.

Creating a more walkable world: "Episode 29: America Walks! w/ Kate Kraft." *Third Wave Urbanism,* Medium, 25 Sept. 2017, https://medium.com/third-wave-urbanism/episode-29-america-walks-w-kate-kraft-891039d0d85b.

"We need a surge": "A People-Centered Transportation System." *Strong Towns,* 27 Oct. 2016, https://www.strongtowns.org/journal/2016/10/27/kate-kraft-america-walks.

STEP 2. PHYSICAL HEALTH

Searching online: "Broken Foot." *WebMD*, 2018, https://www.webmd.com/a-to-z-guides/broken-foot#2.

A HEALTH CRISIS OF EPIDEMIC PROPORTIONS

"America Is Fatter Than Ever": Gardner, Amanda and Healthday Reporter. "Overweight Kids Often Become Obese, Unhealthy Adults." *ABC News,* 23 Mar. 2017, https://abcnews.go.com/Health/Healthday/story?id=4509648&page=1.

An astounding 70 percent: McCarthy, Niall. "U.S. Obesity Rates Have Hit An All-Time High [Infographic]. *Forbes*, 16 Oct. 2017, https://www.forbes.com/sites/sap/2018/07/20/searching-for-the-next-silicon-valley/#7310d9394367.

According to a study: Lee, Bruce. "Seven Misconceptions About the Global Obesity Epidemic." *Forbes,* 28 July 2016, https://www.forbes.com/sites/brucelee/2016/07/28/seven-misconceptions-about-the-global-obesity-epidemic/#59520d232600.

PATIENTS AS PARTNERS

The study, "Patients as Partners": Pomey, Marie-Pascale et al. "Patients as Partners: A Qualitative Study of Patients' Engagement in Their Health Care." Ed. Antony Bayer. *PLoS ONE*10.4 (2015): e0122499. *PMC,* https://www.ncbi.nlm.nih.gov/pmc/articles/PMC4391791/.

TOTAL HEALTH

According to the Center's website: "Kaiser Permanente Center for Total Health." *Kaiser Permanente*, 2018, https://centerfortotalhealth.org.

Instead, a portion of their compensation: Kocher, Dr. Bob. "How 10 Leading Health Systems Pay Their Doctors." *Venrock*, 17 Dec. 2014, https://www.venrock.com/how-10-leading-health-systems-pay-their-doctors/.

In keeping with this mission: Versel, Neil. "Kaiser Permanente Center for Total Health Evolves as Health Care Changes." *MedCityNews*, 15 Sept. 2016, https://medcitynews.com/2016/09/kaiser-center-total-health/.

WALKING AWAY THE HEALTH PROBLEMS

"Walking is a simple way": "New Features Take Kaiser Permanente's Walking App a Step Forward." *Kaiser Permanente*, 4 Mar. 2013, https://share.kaiserpermanente.org/article/new-features-take-kaiser-permanentes-walking-app-a-step-forward/.

From diabetes, depression: Doherty, Trish M. "Join the Walking Revolution!" *Kaiser Permanente Center for Total Health*, 9 June 2014, https://centerfortotalhealth.org/join-the-walking-revolution/.

While type 2 diabetes alone: Walljasper, Jay. "A New Movement Champions Walking for Health and Happiness." *Project for Public Spaces*, 9 Dec. 2013, https://www.pps.org/article/a-new-movement-champions-walking-for-health-and-happiness.

"There's no guarantee": "George C. Halvorson on the Gift of Walking." *Kaiser Permanente Thrive,* YouTube, 16 Jan. 2013, https://www.youtube.com/watch?v=BXx8ABlA6pY.

"A 30-minute walk": Hallett, Vicky. "A Walk with Doc: Surgeon General Regina Benjamin's Walk the Nation Series." *The Washington Post,* 7 June 2010, https://www.washingtonpost.com/express/wp/2010/06/08/walk-the-nation-surgeon-general-dr-regina-benjamin/?utm_term=.abab3d9b08a4.

A STEP IN THE RIGHT DIRECTION

Regardless of how much: "Who We Are." *Walk with a Doc,* 2018, https://walkwithadoc.org/who-we-are/.

The Walk with a Doc website: "Steve Sharp: Dallas, Texas." *Walk with a Doc,* 2018, https://walkwithadoc.org.

A GATEWAY DRUG

ACE's goal is to put people: "About ACE." *The American Council on Exercise,* 2018, https://www.acefitness.org/about-ace/.

They get wrapped up: Waehner, Paige. "Top 10 Reasons You Don't Exercise." *VeryWellFit,* 7 June 2018, https://www.verywellfit.com/top-reasons-you-dont-exercise-1229759.

STEP 3. MENTAL WELLBEING

"If there were a pill": Doherty, Trish M. "Join the Walking Revolution!" *Kaiser Permanente Center for Total Health,* 9 June 2014, https://centerfortotalhealth.org/join-the-walking-revolution/.

Worldwide, nearly one billion people: Ritchie, Hannah and

Max Roser. "Mental Health." *Our World in Data,* April 2018, https://ourworldindata.org/mental-health.

In the United States alone: "Mental Health by the Numbers." *National Alliance on Mental Illness,* 2018, https://www.nami. org/learn-more/mental-health-by-the-numbers.

According to *The American Journal:* Insel, T.R. "Assessing the Economic Costs of Serious Mental Illness." *The American Journal of Psychiatry,* 2008.

People with mental health conditions: "35th Annual Report to Congress on the Implementation of the *Individuals with Disabilities Education Act,* 2013." *U.S. Department of Education,* 2013, https://www2.ed.gov/about/reports/annual/osep/2013/ parts-b-c/35th-idea-arc.pdf.

Suicide is the leading cause: "Children and Mental Health." *Profiles in Science: U.S. National Library of Medicine,* 21 Sept. 2017, https://profiles.nlm.nih.gov/ps/access/NNBBJC.pdf.

In 2015, only 40 percent: "Behavioral Health Trends in the United States: Results from the 2014 National Survey on Drug Use and Health." *Substance Abuse and Mental Health Services Administration,* Sept. 2015, https://www.samhsa.gov/data/sites/ default/files/NSDUH-FRR1-2014/NSDUH-FRR1-2014.pdf.

OVERWORKED + UNDERWALKED

In 2014, 30 percent of college students: Holmes, Lindsay. "19 Statistics That Prove Mental Illness Is More Prominent Than You Think." *HuffPost,* 1 Dec. 2014, https://www.huffingtonpost. com/2014/12/01/mental-illness-statistics_n_6193660.html.

A study from the University of Illinois: University of Illinois at Urbana-Champaign. "Brief Diversions Vastly Improve Focus, Researchers Find." *ScienceDaily*, 8 Feb. 2011, www.sciencedaily.com/releases/2011/02/110208131529.htm.

"Standing up and walking around": Reynolds, Gretchen. "Work. Walk 5 Minutes. Work." *The New York Times,* 28 Dec. 2016, https://www.nytimes.com/2016/12/28/well/move/work-walk-5-minutes-work.html?smprod=nytcore-iphone&smid=nytcore-iphone-share.

"Downtime replenishes the brain's stores": Jabr, Ferris. "Why Your Brain Needs More Downtime." *Scientific American,* 15 Oct. 2013, https://www.scientificamerican.com/article/mental-downtime/.

WALK IT OUT

According to researchers at New Mexico Highlands University: Experimental Biology 2017. "How Walking Benefits the Brain." *Neuroscience News,* 24 Apr. 2017, https://neurosciencenews.com/neurobiology-walking-6487/.

In layman's terms, transient hypofrontality: Dietrich, Arne. "Transient Hypofrontality as a Mechanism for the Psychological Effects of Exercise." *Psychiatry Research,* vol. 145, no. 1, 29 Nov. 2006, pp. 79-83. *Science Direct,* https://doi.org/10.1016/j.psychres.2005.07.033.

On top of those benefits: Breene, Sophia. "13 Mental Health Benefits of Exercise." *HuffPost,* 27 Mar. 2013, https://www.

huffingtonpost.com/2013/03/27/mental-health-benefits-exercise_n_2956099.html.

A WALK IN THE PARK

In the study, Dr. Roe: "Walking Through Green Space Could Help Put Brain In State of Meditation, Study Finds." *HuffPost,* 29 Mar. 2013, https://www.huffingtonpost.com/2013/03/29/green-space-meditation-brain-walk-park_n_2964199.html.
When the volunteers were walking: Reynolds, Gretchen. "Easing Brain Fatigue With a Walk in the Park." *The New York Times,* 27 Mar. 2013, https://well.blogs.nytimes.com/2013/03/27/easing-brain-fatigue-with-a-walk-in-the-park/.
The researchers evaluated the affective: Bratman, Gregory et al. "The Benefits of Nature Experience: Improved Affect and Cognition." *Landscape and Urban Planning,* vol. 138, June 2015, pp. 41-50. *Science Direct,* https://doi.org/10.1016/j.landurbplan.2015.02.005.
The nature walkers also experienced: "Gregory Bratman of Stanford University Describes Environmental Impacts on Mood and Cognition." *Texan by Nature,* YouTube, 12 Sept. 2016, https://www.youtube.com/watch?v=ci6lw8hm9Kk.
While wealthier individuals often experience: Graham, Carol. "The High Costs of Being Poor in America: Stress, Pain, and Worry." *The Brookings Institution,* 19 Feb. 2015, https://www.brookings.edu/blog/social-mobility-memos/2015/02/19/the-high-costs-of-being-poor-in-america-stress-pain-and-worry/.

STEP 4. EMPATHY + UNDERSTANDING

"I was taught to hate Palestinians": Ita Skoblinski, Osnat. "I Was Taught to Hate Palestinians — Until I Met One." *+972 Magazine,* 16 Aug. 2018, https://972mag.com/i-was-taught-to-hate-palestinians-until-i-met-one/128364/.

In October 2017, more than 30,000: Khalkhali, Loubna. "Palestinian and Israeli Woman Walking Hand in Hand For Peace." *MVSLIM.COM,* Nov. 2017, http://mvslim.com/palestinian-and-israeli-women-walking-hand-in-hand-for-peace/.

A TALE OF TWO CITIES

"Washington is known to be deeply divided": "A Tour of a Changing Capital." *The Economist,* 12 Jan. 2017, https://www.economist.com/books-and-arts/2017/01/12/a-tour-of-a-changing-capital.

EXPERIENCING HOMELESSNESS

As of January 2016, there were more: Weiland, Noah. "D.C. Homelessness Doubles National Average as Living Costs Soar." *The New York Times,* 1 Jan. 2017, https://www.nytimes.com/2017/01/01/us/washington-dc-homelessness-double-national-average.html.

These figures illustrate yet another: DeBonis, Mike. "Report: D.C. Is Among Most Unequal Cities by Income." *The Washington Post,* 13 Mar. 2014, https://www.washingtonpost.com/blogs/mike-debonis/wp/2014/03/13/report-d-c-is-among-most-unequal-u-s-cities-by-income/?utm_term=.d14d782d1b79.

"Homelessness knows no race": Covitz, Sydney. "These 10

Graphs Expose D.C.'s Homeless Crisis." *Street Sense Media,* 29 June 2017, https://www.streetsensemedia.org/homeless-ness-washington-dc-statistics-numbers/#.W3TgWC2ZM1h.

Instrumental in this is the Housing First: "Resources: Housing First." *National Alliance to End Homelessness,* 20 Apr. 2016, https://endhomelessness.org/resource/housing-first/.

WALK TOGETHER

"Most of my adult life": Francis, John. *Planetwalker: How to Change Your World One Step at a Time.* Elephant Mountain Press, 2005.

In his TED Talk, "Walk the Earth": Francis, John. "Walk the Earth ... My 17-Year Vow of Silence." *TED: Ideas Worth Spreading,* 2008, https://www.ted.com/talks/john_francis_walks_the_earth/discussion.

Inspired by his journey: "Mission." *Planetwalk,* 2017, http://planetwalk.org/mission/.

A PILGRIM'S JOURNEY

Jason Nellis' post on Medium: "Day 0." *Medium,* 1 June 2016, https://medium.com/@jasonnellis/day-0-1fb697997269.

First popularized during the Middle Ages: "El Camino de Santiago, The Way of St. James." *Camino de Santiago de Compostela,* 2018, https://www.caminosantiagodecompostela.com.

In one of Professor Badone's research studies: Badone, Ellen. "Afterword." *Religion and Society,* 1 Sept. 2014, https://doi.org/10.3167/arrs.2014.050113.

For Jews, Jerusalem is the capital: "Jerusalem." *See the Holy Land*, 2018, http://www.seetheholyland.net/jerusalem/.

While the Middle East remains: "The Holy Land: Jews, Christians and Muslims." *Israel Ministry of Tourism*, Israel Ministry of Foreign Affairs, 2008, http://mfa.gov.il/MFA_Graphics/MFA%20Gallery/Israel60/ch6.pdf.

"Numerous emperors like Charlemagne": "El Camino de Santiago, The Way of St. James." *Camino de Santiago de Compostela*, 2018, https://www.caminosantiagodecompostela.com.

STEP 5. POWER TO THE PEDESTRIANS

242 miles: "Mahatma Gandhi Biography." *Biography.com,* 2018, https://www.biography.com/people/mahatma-gandhi-9305898.

Committed to living a simple life: Sharma, Garvita. "7 Inspiring Facts about Gandhi." *Entertainment Times of India,* 2 Oct. 2015, https://timesofindia.indiatimes.com/life-style/spotlight/7-Inspiring-facts-about-Gandhi/articleshow/49192789.cms.

Although a long geographic distance: Shedden, David. "Today in Media History: In 1930, the Press Reported on Mahatma Gandhi's Salt March." *Poynter*, 12 Mar. 2015, https://www.poynter.org/news/today-media-history-1930-press-reported-mahatma-gandhis-salt-march.

Upon arriving in Dandi: Andrews, Evan. "Remembering Gandhi's Salt March." *History.com,* 12 Mar. 2015, https://www.history.com/news/gandhis-salt-march-85-years-ago.

While the salt laws were by no means: Simon, Johnny and Benjamin Landy. "Gandhi's Salt March: The Nonviolent Journey that Changed the World." *MSNBC*, 16 Mar. 2015, http://www.msnbc.com/msnbc/inside-gandhis-salt-march-the-nonviolent-journey-changed-the-world#slide1.

Although India remained a British colony: "Salt March." *History.com*, 2018, https://www.history.com/topics/salt-march.

MAKING HERSTORY

"Don't get frustrated, get involved": Mckenzie, Joi-Marie. "10 Empowering Quotes from Women's March on Washington." *ABCNews*, 21 Jan. 2017, https://abcnews.go.com/Entertainment/10-empowering-quotes-womens-march-washington/story?id=44948631.

"So many people binge-watch television": Aretakis, Rachel. "Muhammad Ali's Daughter: 'Don't Boo, Vote.'" *Courier Journal,* 21 Jan. 2017, https://www.courier-journal.com/story/news/politics/2017/01/21/muhammad-alis-daughter-dont-boo-vote/96888656/.

The throngs of people are gathered: "Our Mission." *Women's March*, 2018, https://www.womensmarch.com/mission/.

"We're still here": @womensmarch. "We're still here. We're not going anywhere." *Twitter*, https://twitter.com/womensmarch.

After stumbling upon the Women's March: Butler, Breanne. "Smart Cookies and the Legacy of the Women's March." *Cherry Bombe*, 2018, https://cherrybombe.com/86-this/breanne-butler.

While the 2017 marches in Los Angeles: Kassam, Ashifa.

"Nova Scotia Village with 65 Residents Holds One of the Smallest Women's Marches." *The Guardian*, 24 Jan. 2017, https://www.theguardian.com/world/2017/jan/24/nova-scotia-smallest-womens-march-sandy-cove-canada.

From the perspective of economic accessibility: Rogers, Katie. "Amid Division, a March in Washington Seeks to Bring Women Together." *The New York Times*, 18 Nov. 2016, https://www.nytimes.com/2016/11/19/us/womens-march-on-washington.html.

"We're focused on inclusion": Livingston, Eve. "An Organizer of the Women's March Reflects on the World a Year On." *Dazed*, 21 Jan. 2018, http://www.dazeddigital.com/politics/article/38734/1/an-organiser-of-the-womens-march-reflects-on-the-world-a-year-on.

TAKE A WALK. JOIN A MOVEMENT.

"Why are black women dying": Dixon, T. Morgan and Vanessa Garrison. "The Trauma of Systematic Racism is Killing Black Women. A First Step Toward Change..." *TED: Ideas Worth Spreading*, 2017, https://www.ted.com/talks/t_morgan_dixon_and_vanessa_garrison_walking_as_a_revolutionary_act_of_self_care/up-next.

Vanessa's grandmother died: Peters, Adele. "GirlTrek Has a Simple Health Intervention for Black Women: Walking." *Fast Company*, 26 Apr. 2017, https://www.fastcompany.com/40412523/girl-trek-has-a-simple-health-intervention-for-black-women-walking.

Meanwhile, 53 percent of black women: Berger, Erin. "The Trailblazers: Morgan Dixon and Vanessa Garrison." *Outside*, Mariah Media Network LLC, 11 Apr. 2017, https://www.outsideonline.com/2169256/trailblazers-morgan-dixon-and-vanessa-garrison.

Determined to change these statistics: "Vanessa Garrison." *TED: Ideas Worth Spreading*, 2018, https://www.ted.com/speakers/vanessa_garrison.

"For black women whose bodies": Dixon, T. Morgan and Vanessa Garrison. "The Trauma of Systematic Racism is Killing Black Women. A First Step Toward Change..." *TED: Ideas Worth Spreading*, 2017, https://www.ted.com/talks/t_morgan_dixon_and_vanessa_garrison_walking_as_a_revolutionary_act_of_self_care/up-next.

Susie Page, a Philadelphia resident: "Have You Heard of GirlTrek? You Can Thank Us Later." *Philly Powered*, 20 June 2016, http://phillypowered.org/heard-girltrek-thank-us-later/.

The Project for Public Spaces concurs: Walljasper, Jay. "A New Movement Champions Walking for Health and Happiness." *Project for Public Spaces*, 9 Dec. 2013, https://www.pps.org/article/a-new-movement-champions-walking-for-health-and-happiness.

HOW MOVEMENTS HAPPEN

"People always say": Johnson, Steven. "My Life Since the

2012 Sandy Hook Shooting: Sarah Clements's Story." *The Atlantic*, 24 Mar. 2018, https://www.theatlantic.com/family/archive/2018/03/sarah-clements/556355/.

The organizers have developed: *March for Our Lives*, 2018, https://marchforourlives.com.

STEP 6. WALKING FOR A CAUSE

Cancer is one of the leading causes: "Cancer Statistics." *National Cancer Institute*, 2018, https://www.cancer.gov/about-cancer/understanding/statistics.

Every 98 seconds, an American: "Victims of Sexual Violence: Statistics." *RAINN*, 2018, https://www.rainn.org/statistics/victims-sexual-violence.

More than 750 million people: "11 Facts About Global Poverty." *DoSomething.org*, 2018, https://www.dosomething.org/us/facts/11-facts-about-global-poverty.

WALK FOR LIFE

Relay for Life's founder: "Learn About Relay." *The American Cancer Society*, 2018, https://secure.acsevents.org/site/SPageServer?pagename=relay_learn.

As of 2018, Relay for Life has raised: "Mission Statement." *The American Cancer Society*, 12 Jan. 2017, https://www.cancer.org/about-us/who-we-are/mission-statements.html.

In his TED Talk "Are you a giver or a taker?": Grant, Adam. "Are You a Giver or a Taker?" *TED: Ideas Worth Spreading*, 24 Jan. 2017, https://www.youtube.com/watch?v=YyXRYgjQXX0.

"Cancer patients don't stop": "Learn About Relay." *The American Cancer Society*, 2018, https://secure.acsevents.org/site/SPageServer?pagename=relay_learn.

FIGHTING CANCER IS A MARATHON, NOT A SPRINT

Each year, the walk — now called "AVON 39": *AVON 39: The Walk to End Breast Cancer*, 2018, http://www.avon39.org.
"A large piece of the money stays": "Why We Walk: AVON 39: The Walk to End Breast Cancer." *Avon Breast Cancer Crusade*, 2018, https://avonbcc.org/avon39-walk/.
This time, Academy Award-winning actress: Witherspoon, Reese. "Reese Witherspoon: 'Anyone is Susceptible' to Breast Cancer." *CNN Entertainment*, 12 Sept. 2008, http://www.cnn.com/2008/SHOWBIZ/09/11/reese.avon.walk/index.html.

WALK A MILE IN THEIR SHOES

"Move your hips and swing your arms": "Instructions for Walking." *Walk a Mile in Her Shoes*, 2017, http://www.walkamileinhershoes.org/Walk_Event_Experience/instructionswalk.html#.W3T2Vi2ZM1h.
While the event's execution is indeed humorous: "Welcome." *Walk a Mile in Her Shoes*, 2017, http://www.walkamileinhershoes.org.
The Project Concern International (PCI) Walk for Water: Gauss, Allison. "4 Lessons from the Best Charity Run/Walks." *Classy*, 2018, https://www.classy.org/blog/4-lessons-best-charity-runwalks/.

Women in developing countries spend: Costanza, Kari. "Melinda Gates on What Faith in Action Means to Her." *World Vision,* 3 Nov. 2016, https://www.worldvision.org/gender-equality-news-stories/melinda-gates-interview.

While the Walk for Water course: Finn, Stephen. "Walk for Water with Mark Mullen on March 20th." *NBC San Diego,* 7 Mar. 2011, https://www.nbcsandiego.com/on-air/community/Walk-for-Water-On-March-20th-117548968.html.

Still, it helps bridge: "Showers." *HomeWaterWorks,* 2018, https://www.home-water-works.org/indoor-use/showers.

"When you ask public health experts": "A Walk to Remember: PCI Hosts 10th Annual Walk for Water." *PCI Global,* 2 May 2018, https://www.pciglobal.org/a-walk-for-water-to-remember/.

In 2016, for example, PCI partnered: "Tackling Ethiopia's Water Crisis with Partnership." *PCI Global,* 26 Aug. 2016, https://www.pciglobal.org/tackling-ethiopias-water-crisis-with-partnership/.

STEP 7. THE FOOTPRINT WE LEAVE

We're in "uncharted territory": Plummer, Libby and Cara McGoogan. "11 Terrifying Climate Change Facts." *Wired,* 4 Sept. 2017, https://www.wired.co.uk/article/climate-change-facts.

Although the world's wealthiest countries: Althor, Glenn, James E. M. Watson, and Richard A. Fuller. "Global Mismatch Between Greenhouse Gas Emissions and the Burden of Climate Change." *Scientific Reports* 6, 2016, doi: 10.1038/srep20281.

Not only does the burden: "The Impact of Climate Change

on the Vulnerability of the Poor." *Department for International Development*, 2004, https://www.unpei.org/sites/default/files/PDF/resourceefficiency/KM-resource-DFID-impact-climat-echange-vulnerability.pdf.

Since 2008, an annual average: "Frequently Asked Questions on Climate Change and Disaster Displacement." *UNHCR: The UN Refugee Agency,* 6 Nov. 2016, http://www.unhcr.org/uk/news/latest/2016/11/581f52dc4/frequently-asked-questions-climate-change-disaster-displacement.html.

It's no wonder that nearly half: Loudenback, Tanza and Abby Jackson. "The 10 Most Critical Problems in the World, According to Millennials." *Business Insider,* 26 Feb. 2018, https://www.businessinsider.com/world-economic-forum-world-biggest-problems-concerning-millennials-2016-8.

Amid the climate crisis: Lee, Ga Ram. "Al Gore Educates Georgetown Students on Climate Crisis." *The Caravel,* 25 Apr. 2018, http://gucaravel.com/al-gore-educates-georgetown-students-climate-crisis/.

THE NATURAL CHOICE

About 70 percent of all car trips: "Who's Walking and Bicycling." *Pedestrian and Bicycle Information,* U.S. Department of Transportation, 2018, http://www.pedbikeinfo.org/data/factsheet_general.cfm.

Car trips of less than a mile: "What If We Kept Our Cars Parked for Trips Less Than One Mile?" *United States Environmental Protection Agency,* 2017, https://www.epa.gov/greenvehicles/

what-if-we-kept-our-cars-parked-trips-less-one-mile.

On foot, the average person: Bumgardner, Wendy. "Walking Time for Distances from a Mile to a Marathon." *Very Well Fit,* 13 Jan. 2018, https://www.verywellfit.com/miles-and-kilometers-how-far-is-that-3435412.

"If we all chose to power": "What If We Kept Our Cars Parked for Trips Less Than One Mile?" *United States Environmental Protection Agency,* 2017, https://www.epa.gov/greenvehicles/what-if-we-kept-our-cars-parked-trips-less-one-mile.

WALK THE EARTH

"Life is hard enough": "Environmentalist John Francis, Walking the Walk." *All Things Considered,* NPR, 24 Apr. 2005, https://www.npr.org/templates/story/story.php?storyId=4616383.

Environment activists tend to "shout": Fromson, Daniel. "A Conversation with John Francis, 'Planetwalker' and Conservationist." *The Atlantic,* 28 Mar. 2011, https://www.theatlantic.com/national/archive/2011/03/a-conversation-with-john-francis-planetwalker-and-conservationist/73126/.

Transect walks are a popular technique: "Community Mapping through Transect Walks." *Catalytic Communities,* 2018, http://catcomm.org/transect-walk/.

When the Exxon Valdez oil spill: Lepisto, Meghan. "Silent for 17 Years, Planetwalker John Francis Lends His Voice as Visiting Professor." *Nelson Institute for Environmental Studies, University of Wisconsin-Madison,* 7 Feb. 2011, http://nelson.wisc.edu/news/story.php?story=1141.

In his TED Talk, "Walk the Earth...": "Walk the Earth ... My 17-Year Vow of Silence." *TED: Ideas Worth Spreading,* 2008, https://www.ted.com/talks/john_francis_walks_the_earth/transcript#t-748650.

THE FOOTPRINT(S) WE LEAVE

The United States government responded: Ross, Michael L. "How the 1973 Oil Embargo Saved the Planet." *Foreign Affairs,* 15 Oct. 2013, https://www.foreignaffairs.com/articles/north-america/2013-10-15/how-1973-oil-embargo-saved-planet.

In 2016, more than 6,000: "Pedestrian and Bicyclist Crash Statistics." *Pedestrian and Bicycle Information,* U.S. Department of Transportation, 2018, http://www.pedbikeinfo.org/data/factsheet_crash.cfm.

To improve safety in the short-term: Plungis, Jeff. "U.S. Traffic Deaths Top 37,000; Pedestrian and Bicycle Deaths Hit Highs." *Consumer Reports,* 7 Oct. 2017, https://www.consumerreports.org/transportation/nhtsa-2016-highway-fatalities/.

In order to ensure long-term: "It's Easy Being Breen: walking vs. Driving Is a No-Brainer." *Center for American Progress,* 2 July 2008, https://www.americanprogress.org/issues/green/news/2008/07/02/4723/its-easy-being-green-walking-vs-driving-is-a-no-brainer/.

Economics professor Richard Mckenzie: Tierney, John. "How Virtuous is Ed Begley Jr." *The New York Times,* 25 Feb. 2008, https://tierneylab.blogs.nytimes.com/2008/02/25/

how-virtuous-is-ed-begley-jr/?scp=1&sq=how%20
virtuous%20is%20ed%20begley&st=cse&mtrref=undefined.

The Institute found that walking: Cohen, Michael and Matthew Heberger. "Driving vs. Waking: Cows, Climate Change, and Choice." *Pacific Institute*, Apr. 2008, http://www.pacinst. org/topics/integrity_of_science/case_studies/driving_vs_ walking.pdf.

When considering the average American: "It's Easy Being Green: Walking vs. Driving Is a No-Brainer." *Center for American Progress,* 2 July 2008, https://www.americanprogress.org/issues/green/news/2008/07/02/4723/ its-easy-being-green-walking-vs-driving-is-a-no-brainer/.

Walking reduces traffic congestion: "Reducing Your Transportation Footprint." *Center for Climate and Energy Solutions*, 2018, https://www.c2es.org/content/ reducing-your-transportation-footprint/.

TAKE A HIKE

Not only does hiking provide: Heid, Markham. "Why Hiking Is the Perfect Mind-Body Workout." *Time,* 5 July 2017, http:// time.com/4820394/hiking-walking-mind-body-workout/.

According to the Stanford University: Bratman, Gregory et al. "Nature Experience Reduces Rumination and Subgenual Prefrontal Cortex Activation." *Proceedings of the National Academy of Sciences of the United States of America,* 14 July 2015, https://doi.org/10.1073/pnas.1510459112.

"Unlike going to the movies": Zak, Emily. "Outdoor

Recreation Isn't Free — Why We Need to Stop Pretending It Is." *Everyday Feminism,* 8 Apr. 2017, https://everydayfeminism. com/2017/04/outdoor-recreation-isnt-free/.

For those pursuing overnight adventures: Kelley, Mark. "How Much Does it Cost to Hike the Appalachian Trail?" *Adventure Possible,* 22 Mar. 2015, http://adventurepossible.com/adventure/ how-much-does-it-cost-to-hike-the-appalachian-trail/.

National park attendance rates reflect: Zak, Emily. "Outdoor Recreation Isn't Free — Why We Need to Stop Pretending It Is." *Everyday Feminism,* 8 Apr. 2017, https://everydayfeminism. com/2017/04/outdoor-recreation-isnt-free/.

"It's hard to see yourself": Berger, Erin. "To Diversify the Outdoors, We Have to Think About Who We're Excluding." *Outside,* 15 Nov. 2016, https://www.outsideonline.com/2131911/ diversify-outdoors-we-have-think-about-who-were-excluding.

Fresh Air Fund: *The Fresh Air Fund,* 2018, http://www.fre-shair.org.

Vida Verde: *Vida Verde Nature Education,* 2018, https://www. vveducation.org.

Outdoor Afro: *Outdoor Afro,* 2018, http://outdoorafro.com/ blog/.

Latino Outdoors: *Latino Outdoors,* 2018, http://latinooutdoors.org.

When it comes to building: Zak, Emily. "Outdoor Recreation Isn't Free — Why We Need to Stop Pretending It Is." *Everyday Feminism,* 8 Apr. 2017, https://everydayfeminism.com/2017/04/ outdoor-recreation-isnt-free/.

STEP 8. THE WALKING ECONOMY

Until the early 20th century: "History of the Automobile." *The University of Colorado Boulder,* 2018, http://l3d.cs.colorado. edu/systems/agentsheets/New-Vista/automobile/.

THE COMEBACK KID

CEOs for Cities, a non-profit: "About CEOs for Cities." *CEOs for Cities,* 2018, https://ceosforcities.org/about/.

To Adam, the Atlanta BeltLine: "The Atlanta BeltLine in 5." *Atlanta BeltLine,* 2018, https://beltline.org/about/ the-atlanta-beltline-project/atlanta-beltline-overview/.

"[Atlanta] residents have a tendency": Serna, Rebecca. "Transforming Atlanta." *Rails to Trails Conservancy,* 21 Apr. 2015, https://www.railstotrails.org/trailblog/2015/april/21/ transforming-atlanta/.

An overwhelming 50 percent of U.S. residents: "Active Transportation and Real Estate: The Next Frontier." *Urban Land Institute,* March 2016, http://uli.org/wp-content/uploads/ ULI-Documents/Active-Transportation-and-Real-Estate-The-Next-Frontier.pdf.

Suburban walking communities positioned: Thompson, Derek and Jordan Weissman. "The Cheapest Generation." *The Atlantic,* Sept. 2012, https://www.theatlantic.com/magazine/ archive/2012/09/the-cheapest-generation/309060/.

By 2014, a former golf course: Scott, Sonny. "NLR to Convert Old Golf Course into Park." *THV11,* 28 Mar. 2016, https://www.thv11.com/article/news/local/

nlr-to-convert-old-golf-course-into-park/106862821.

According to local realtors: KATV. "$40K approved to Turn NLR Golf Course into New Park." *ABC7: KATV Little Rock,* 28 Mar. 2016, https://katv.com/news/local/hundreds-expected-at-satanic-temple-rally-at-ark-capitol-senator-rapert-responds.

In 2009, Albert Lea, a town of 18,000: Stachura, Sea. "Albert Lea Embarks on a Healthy Makeover." *MPR News,* 16 Jan. 2009, https://www.mprnews.org/story/2009/01/15/longevity_albert_lea.

Blue Zones is an organization: *Blue Zones,* 2018, https://www.bluezones.com/#section-1.

The campaign was based: Walljasper, Jay. "Albert Lea Shows How Walking and Other Healthy Habits Can Rejuvenate a Rural Community." *MinnPost,* 22 May 2015, https://www.minnpost.com/health/2015/05/albert-lea-shows-how-walking-and-other-healthy-habits-can-rejuvenate-rural-community.

The shifts to encourage walkability: Wiles, Sam. "It's Official: Albert Lea Certified a Blue Zones City." *Albert Lea Tribune,* 2 Oct. 2016, https://www.albertleatribune.com/2016/10/its-official-albert-lea-certified-a-blue-zones-city/.

When it comes to making the 10-minute walk: Riggs, Trisha. "Nation's Mayors Launch Groundbreaking 10-Minute Walk to a Park Campaign." *Urban Land Institute,* 10 Oct. 2017, https://americas.uli.org/press-release/nations-mayors-launch-groundbreaking-10-minute-walk-park-campaign/.

Constructed in the 1930s: "About the High Line." *Friends of the High Line*, 2018, http://www.thehighline.org/about.

"Once-thriving restaurants": Moss, Jeremiah. "Disney World on the Hudson." *The New York Times*, 21 Aug. 2012, https://www.nytimes.com/2012/08/22/opinion/in-the-shadows-of-the-high-line.html?mtrref=www.google.com&assetType=opinion&mtrref=www.nytimes.com&g-wh=BC4FCAFD209844A188606C2D34267F12&gwt=pay&assetType=opinion.

"We were from the community": Bliss, Laura. "The High Line's Next Balancing Act." *CityLab*, 7 Feb. 2017, https://www.citylab.com/solutions/2017/02/the-high-lines-next-balancing-act-fair-and-affordable-development/515391/.

EQUAL OPPORTUNITY + WALKABLE DESIGN

In 2012, Christopher and his colleague: Alfonzo, Mariela and Christopher B. Leinberger. "Walk this Way: The Economic Promise of Walkable Places in Metropolitan Washington, D.C." *The Brookings Institution*, 25 May 2012, https://www.brookings.edu/research/walk-this-waythe-economic-promise-of-walkable-places-in-metropolitan-washington-d-c/.

"The pace at which Milan intends": O'Sullivan, Feargus. "The Plan to Pedestrianize Central Milan." *CityLab*, 13 July 2015, https://www.citylab.com/transportation/2015/07/the-plan-to-pedestrianize-central-milan/398387/.

In the field of urban planning: "Devon McAslan: Current

Student — Ph.D. in Urban and Regional Planning." *University of Michigan Taubman College*, 2018, https://taubmancollege.umich.edu/urbanplanning/students/student-work/phd-urban-planning/devon-mcaslan.

STEP 9. NEXT STEPS

THE SECRET TO GREATER PRODUCTIVITY

Walking together also stimulates: Williams, Lawrence E. and John A. Bargh. "Experiencing Physical Warmth Promotes Interpersonal Warmth." *Science,* vol. 322, 24 Oct. 2008, pp. 606-607, https://doi.org/10.1126/science.1162548.

Ted was scheduled to present: "DC Walking Summit: Ted Eytan." *EveryBodyWalk*, YouTube, 21 Jan. 2014, https://www.youtube.com/watch?v=ON_KBZygHlo.

A CREATIVITY BOOST

"There is something truly compelling": Fishbane, Lara. "What is the Crux of Blockchain?" *Beeck Center for Social Impact + Innovation at Georgetown University*, 22 Jan. 2018, http://beeckcenter.georgetown.edu/crux-blockchain/.

Marily Oppezzo, a researcher: Oppezzo, Marily. "Want to Be More Creative? Go For a Walk." *TED: Ideas Worth Spreading*, 2018, https://www.ted.com/talks/marily_oppezzo_want_to_be_more_creative_go_for_a_walk/discussion.

"Sitting can kill you": Scutti, Susan. "Yes, Sitting Too Long

Can Kill You, Even If You Exercise." *CNN*, 12 Sept. 2017, https://www.cnn.com/2017/09/11/health/sitting-increases-risk-of-death-study/index.html.

THE MOST POWERFUL PEOPLE ARE PEDESTRIANS

Albert Einstein, the father: Gorvett, Zaria. "What You Can Learn from Einstein's Quirky Habits." *BBC*, 12 June 2017, http://www.bbc.com/future/story/20170612-what-you-can-learn-from-einsteins-quirky-habits.

Henry David Thoreau, a 19th-century: Thoreau, Henry David. "Walking." *The Atlantic*, June 1862, https://www.theatlantic.com/magazine/archive/1862/06/walking/304674/.

Michelle and Barack Obama, one of the: "The World's Most Powerful Couples." *Forbes*, 2018, https://www.forbes.com/pictures/eikf45kgj/michelle-and-barack-obama/#3b47e8757e91.

As the 44th President of the United States: Herman, Ryan. "Walk and Talk: Why Walking Meetings Make Business Sense." *Director*, 3 June 2016, https://www.director.co.uk/walking-meetings-make-business-sense-18387-2/.

On one occasion, he went: "Angela Merkel and Barack Obama's German Breakfast Meeting — In Pictures." *The Guardian*, 7 June 2015, https://www.theguardian.com/us-news/gallery/2015/jun/07/angela-merkel-barack-obama-breakfast-meeting-pictures.

At home in the United States: Leonnig, Carol D. "Obama's Stroll is No Walk In the Park for Secret Service." *The Washington Post*, 23 May 2014, https://www.washingtonpost.com/

news/post-politics/wp/2014/05/23/obamas-stroll-is-no-walk-in-the-park-for-secret-service/?utm_term=.31b7b4b52d3c.

As the First Lady of the United States: Harrington, Elizabeth. "Michelle Obama Gives a Nod to 'Walking School Buses.'" *CNSNews.com*, 15 July 2013, https://www.cnsnews.com/news/article/michelle-obama-gives-nod-walking-school-buses.

Steve Jobs, CEO of Apple: Hayes, Julian. "Steve Jobs' 1 Simple Habit to Boost Happiness, Productivity, and Creativity." *Inc.*, 30 Nov. 2017, https://www.inc.com/hrci/inclusive-talent-management-an-overview.html.

"If there was something that Steve": Hesseldahl, Arik. "Larry Ellison Talked About a Long Hike with Steve Jobs in USC's Commencement Speech." *Recode*, 13 May 2016, https://www.recode.net/2016/5/13/11672932/larry-ellison-steve-jobs-oracle-apple-usc.

When it came to meeting new people: Tate, Andrew. "Why Everyone from Beethoven, Goethe, Dickens, Darwin to Steve Jobs Took Long Walks and Why You Should Too." *Canva*, 2018, https://www.canva.com/learn/taking-long-walks/.

Following in the footsteps of Steve Jobs: Kirkpatrick, David. "How Facebook's Mark Zuckerberg Changed the World." *Daily Nation*, 24 Dec. 2010, https://www.nation.co.ke/business/Tech/How-Facebooks-Mark-Zuckerberg-changed-the-world/1017288-1078124-9yoa5y/index.html.

After a series of hour-long walks: Talev, Margaret and Carol Hymowitz. "Executives Say Walking During Meetings Leads to Good Decision-Making."

Mashable, 30 Apr. 2014, https://mashable.com/2014/04/30/walking-meetings-decision-making/#p_Ix5xfzxaqF.

In another walking meeting with Facebook: Shriar, Jacob. "Reasons Why You Need To Have Walking Meetings." *OfficeVibe*, 29 Mar. 2014, https://www.officevibe.com/blog/walking-meetings-employee-wellness.

On a few occasions, Steve Jobs: Mitchell, Dan. "Silicon Valley's Different Kind of Power Walk." *Fortune*, 16 Nov. 2011, http://fortune.com/2011/11/15/silicon-valleys-different-kind-of-power-walk/.

Nilofer Merchant's 2013 TED Talk: Merchant, Nilofer. "Got a Meeting? Take a Walk." *TED: Ideas Worth Spreading*, 2013, https://www.ted.com/talks/nilofer_merchant_got_a_meeting_take_a_walk/up-next.

ENVISIONING CHANGE

The process of Milan's pedestrianization: ARUP. "Cities Alive: Towards a Walking World." *ARUP*, June 2016, http://www.walkdvrc.hk/upload/files/research/20170818143200_40.pdf.

ACKNOWLEDGEMENTS

———

To all of the people who walked with me throughout the adventure of writing my first book, I cannot begin to thank you enough.

Words cannot express my gratitude to my family for your unwavering love and support. To my parents, who taught me how to walk, thank you for inspiring me to believe in my ability to change the world. To my brother, John, thank you for for sharing your creative mind with me and for challenging me to be a better person every day.

This book would not have been possible without the guidance and wisdom of all of my interviewees. Thank you for taking the time to share your worldview with me and for giving me a glimpse into the incredible good that walking is already doing in the world.

I am immensely grateful to my friends for walking through life with me — both literally and figuratively. Thank you for agreeing to go on some pretty crazy walking adventures with me and for offering endless support and enthusiasm throughout the highs and lows of the writing process. Special thanks to Abby Reinhold, Greer Richey, and Nina Lund-Simon for being the most brilliant team of pre-readers that I could have asked for.

Last but certainly not least, I am eternally grateful to the New Degree Press team — especially Eric Koester, Brian Bies, and Anastasia Armendariz — for walking me through the process of turning my big idea into a reality. Without you, this book would still be a bunch of unorganized thoughts floating around in my head.

42795722R00168

Made in the USA
Middletown, DE
17 April 2019